FEMINISM
IN MINUTES

FEMINISM IN MINUTES

SHANNON WEBER

Quercus

Contents

Introduction

Feminism as a Western political movement began during the 19th century. Since that time myriad topics have fallen within its scope and all sorts of diverse movements have mobilized under – and in tension with – its banner. While some people have forged fierce resistance to its messages, others devote their entire lives to feminism, sometimes even dying for it. In numerous ways, its past implicates our present… and our future.

This book chronicles feminism from its origins as a 19th-century political movement, while also taking a wider view, understanding that the fight for women's freedom goes back much further. In this book you'll find all sorts of subjects covered, from textbook feminist icons to the movements you were never taught about at school. Whether you're just learning about feminism or want more ideas and perspectives, this book is for you!

Chapters are organized by topic to help you make connections and identify themes. However, many of the ideas discussed here are multi-dimensional, and could easily fit into more than one chapter. For example, many indigenous women are fighting for their families, for racial justice and sexual and reproductive freedom and against colonization and poverty all at the same time. Because of this, you're encouraged to make connections between chapters.

You'll also notice a chronological order within each chapter. This is to help you see the foundations and evolution of feminist thought and activism. At the same time, feminists keep coming back to several key struggles. You'll see how they've been grinding away against economic oppression from the days of feudalism to Occupy Wall Street, for example, and how they've been fighting for sexual autonomy, respect and their very lives in societies both ancient and modern.

Empires rise and fall. Progress does not occur organically. Justice requires close attention to power and inequality. People in every age must honour the struggles of their ancestors with an eye on the future. This is how feminism continues to change and shape our world. In the words of Indian feminist writer and activist Arundhati Roy, 'Another world is not only possible, she is on her way. On a quiet day, I can hear her breathing.'

Reclaiming women's history

Women have been pivotal to the shaping of world history since the dawn of human existence. However, their contributions and perspectives have frequently been erased while patriarchal viewpoints – masked as neutral tellings of events – have triumphed.

When feminist activists began fighting for women's inclusion in the curricula of higher education in the 1970s, many fields, including history and literature, were dominated by the stories of white men. Feminists sought to remedy this by including novels and poetry by women in English classes and in re-examining history to account for women's narratives.

The early excavations of these stories were referred to by many feminists in the 1970s as 'herstory'. As women entered academia, the shape of human knowledge was enriched and transformed by works about women. This early scholarship formed the core of what would become women's and gender studies.

Detail of musicians and dancers on an ancient Egyptian fresco at the Tomb of Nebamun c. 14th century BCE.

Feminism and language

Feminists have been objecting to male-centred language – for example, the use of 'he' to refer to a person of any gender, calling all of humanity 'mankind' and calling all police officers 'policemen' – since at least the 1960s. In her 1975 paper 'Androcentrism in Proscriptive Grammar', sociologist Anne Bodine discussed the merits of using the singular 'they' pronoun as well as 'he or she' as a suitable replacement for the all-encompassing 'he'. In gendered languages such as French and German, feminists have led efforts since the 1980s to reorient their languages towards becoming non-sexist, with mixed results.

Feminists have also challenged how language is structured. When discussing sexual violence, for example, it is common to say 'She was raped', focusing on the victim while obscuring the perpetrator of the crime. 'Someone raped her', in contrast, puts the onus on the person who committed the crime. Feminist language rejects passive descriptions of oppression, replacing them with those aimed at holding perpetrators accountable.

Sex versus gender

Many people use the terms 'sex' and 'gender' interchangeably. This is understandable, as the terms are used as synonyms in all kinds of contexts, from everyday language to data boxes on official forms. Within a feminist context, however, sex and gender are complex topics that have distinct and different meanings.

'Sex' refers to the physical characteristics of the human body – it concerns that which is biological. The term also recognizes that sex is not always clear-cut, as with intersex people, and has the possibility to change, as with transgender people who may undergo surgery to feel more comfortable in their bodies. 'Gender', meanwhile, constitutes the social meanings mapped onto people's bodies as a result of assumptions about sex. For example, a person with a penis is assumed to be masculine and to enjoy rough activities such as sport. Gender also refers to the way in which a person views themself, regardless of sex; for example, whether they feel masculine, feminine, both or neither based on societal definitions of those terms.

Trans woman and World War II veteran Christine Jorgensen. The first person widely known in the United States to have gender confirmation surgery in the 1950s, Jorgensen challenged society's assumptions about the relationship between sex and gender.

Nature versus nurture

Do people act the way they do because they're biologically hardwired to do so, or because they picked up messages about how to act from their parents, peers, culture, religion and society? Psychologists and sociologists have discussed nature versus nurture for over a hundred years, with diverse results. Many have concluded that it's a mixture of both, while others have argued it's more nature or more nurture.

Feminist thinkers, researchers and activists have been asking these same questions about gender, in turn questioning the received wisdom of their societies. Scientists in the 19th century, for example, tried to argue that women were biologically inferior to men and that their bodies couldn't handle the strain of higher education. In response, many feminist psychologists, sociologists and biologists have written about the ways in which science has been abused to justify the ill treatment of marginalized groups, as well as the ways in which gender norms are socially determined and change over time.

The virgin/whore dichotomy

The virgin/whore dichotomy refers to a sexual double standard in which women are seen as being either virtuous, asexual beings (often in the likeness of the virgin Mary) or as sinful seductresses (in the style of the biblical Jezebel). In popular culture, women and girls are given mixed messages about what they are supposed to aspire to, as they are expected to be sexy yet not 'slutty', the 'girl next door' yet not a 'prude'. Feminists have argued that, as a result of patriarchal societies creating this reductive binary, women are stigmatized no matter how they act, always judged as too sexual or not sexual enough, in a way that heterosexual men and boys aren't forced to experience.

Some theories as to why patriarchal societies have created this dichotomy include the misogynist influence of Judeo-Christian depictions of women. They suggest that men divide women into two groups, one they can respect and love and one they can desire; and that men harbour a deep hatred for women based on childhood experiences with their mothers.

Compulsory heterosexuality

The term 'compulsory heterosexuality' was coined in 1980 by feminist scholar, poet and activist Adrienne Rich. Rich argued that, throughout history, men in patriarchal societies have mandated that women enter into heterosexual matrimony. Fathers and husbands have exchanged women as commodities, and women continue to face various social, legal and economic repercussions if they refuse these unions. Rich argued that heterosexuality is something women have been coercively socialized into from birth. According to Rich, women have the ability to break free from compulsory heterosexuality, specifically in pursuing relationships with other women, both sexual and non-sexual. She referred to the spectrum of possible relationships between women as the 'lesbian continuum'. The argument that any woman can abandon heterosexuality and 'choose' to invest their energies in other women was controversial even among other feminists and lesbians; however, it was a central tenet of 1970s and 1980s radical lesbian feminism.

Privilege and oppression

Privilege and oppression are key concepts in feminism. 'Privilege' refers to the unearned advantages a person has at birth and that accumulate over time. 'Oppression', meanwhile, refers to the ways in which a person is treated poorly and denied resources due to their social position. Systems of oppression privilege people with power at the expense of those without. A person can be simultaneously privileged and oppressed – say, someone who is both white and poor. In 1989, white feminist scholar and activist Peggy McIntosh wrote a classic article called 'White Privilege: Unpacking the Invisible Knapsack'. McIntosh used the metaphor of the invisible knapsack to explain how white people are born with various 'tools' that aid them in life, tools unavailable to people of colour. Her examples ranged from her children being taught in school about the historical achievements of mostly white people to being able to find plasters matching her skin colour at the supermarket. Taking accountable action for one's privilege is something that remains a challenge for many feminist movements.

Elizabeth Eckford, one of the nine African American students enrolled in Little Rock Central High during the early effort to desegregate it, is harassed on the first day of school in September 1957. Arkansas National Guards were ineffective in controlling racist crowds and were replaced by Federal troops.

Intersectionality

Intersectionality asks the simple question: which women are we talking about? In the 1970s, while feminist movements dominated by white women with class privilege were bonding over how 'sisterhood is powerful', many 'sisters' who experienced oppression for reasons other than gender were made to feel like outsiders. These included women of colour and poor and working-class women of all ethnicities.

US legal scholar Kimberlé Crenshaw coined the term 'intersectionality' in 1991 to demonstrate how women of colour experience oppression. The theory suggests that systems of oppression are both multiple – based on race, gender, class and more – and interlocking: women of colour don't experience racism *and* sexism. Rather, they experience racism that is sexualized, sexism that is racialized, and often classism that is filtered through both a racist and sexist lens. These systems of oppression are perpetuated through institutions like government, media and the legal system.

Kimberlé Crenshaw

The myth of meritocracy

The theory of meritocracy means that success is determined by one's merit, not by birth or connections. In the United States, this theory is connected to the idea of the 'American dream', where ambition will be rewarded with a prosperous life, no matter where you come from. In reality, some groups of people (such as women of colour, queer and trans women, poor women and disabled women) are born with far fewer resources and poorer societal treatment than others and it's harder for them to become financially prosperous than it is for others. In the case of oppression, the failure to succeed may not necessarily be tied to a person's merit, but to factors beyond their control. Given the realities of housing and job discrimination, racial profiling, lack of access to intergenerational wealth-building for indigenous and black people as a result of genocide and slavery, and more, feminists often argue that meritocracy is a myth. This myth justifies the continued oppression of marginalized groups while enabling those groups to be blamed for their own oppression via harmful stereotypes.

The feminization of poverty

American researcher Diana Pearce coined the concept 'the feminization of poverty' in 1978, as a way to describe how a disproportionately high number of women around the globe live in poverty due to misogyny (and often other forms of discrimination such as racism, ableism and ageism). Pearce argued that while US women gained some independence from men, beginning in the 1950s through paid employment and divorce, women's financial independence has continued to lag far behind due to being paid lower wages.

The gender wage gap is intensified for women of colour, most of whom are paid less than white men or women. According to one 2014 US study, for every dollar white men earned, white women earned approximately $.75, black women earned $.61, indigenous and Asian Pacific Islander women earned $.59, and Latina women earned $.55. For households headed by female couples, the negative impact of the wage gap is doubled.

Photojournalist Dorothea Lange's 1936 *Migrant Mother* depicts Cherokee mother Florence Leona Thompson struggling to survive with three of her children in California. The image became an iconic symbol of the US Great Depression.

Media and the male gaze

The idea of the male gaze has its roots in a 1975 essay on classical Hollywood cinema by feminist film theorist Laura Mulvey. Mulvey used psychoanalysis to argue that in these films, the (male) filmmaker used the camera to reflect heterosexual male desire, assuming that the viewer would also be a heterosexual man. The filmmaker would divide a woman's body into parts instead of showing her as a whole, then zoom in on her, scanning up her body in a sexualizing manner. While men in classical Hollywood were shown as complex subjects, women were routinely portrayed as eroticized props for men's consumption. Mulvey used Sigmund Freud's theory of scopophilia – the pleasure gained through looking – to argue that women's 'to-be-looked-at-ness', as she put it, constituted a form of voyeurism.

Today, the theory of the male gaze continues to inform how feminists analyze the representation of women in media, as well as discussions of street harassment, rape culture and other types of sexual objectification of women.

A man looks up the skirt of the famous *Forever Marilyn* statue designed by artist Seward Johnson, shown here on display in Palm Springs, California.

Racist tropes and controlling media images

While white women have had to contend with sexually objectifying and demeaning portrayals in media, women of colour have had to deal with concerns based not only on sexism, but also racism. Vastly underrepresented, women of colour have often been limited to racist and sexist stereotypes in supporting roles, such as the enslaved black 'mammy' cheerfully taking care of white children, or the Latina maid.

Feminist sociologist Patricia Hill Collins wrote about these dynamics in her 1990 book *Black Feminist Thought*, in which she described the 'controlling images' of black women as reinforcing black women's social status as 'other'. Controlling images of black women, Collins wrote, include the mammy, the matriarch, the black lady and the jezebel. Each of these images have real-world impacts on black women's daily lives; for example, Collins cites black feminist writer and activist Audre Lorde's anecdote of a young white girl pointing at Lorde's toddler daughter at the supermarket and calling her a 'baby maid'.

Vivien Leigh and Hattie McDaniel in *Gone with the Wind* (1939).

The beauty myth

Tying a woman's value to her beauty is inextricably linked to the sexual objectification of women. In the 19th century, men tried to control women's political power by dismissing suffragists as ugly and unwomanly. In 1990, feminist journalist Naomi Wolf wrote *The Beauty Myth*. Wolf argued that, as women made more professional and legal gains over the 20th century, they've been held to increasingly impossible standards of beauty, defined so narrowly that these ideals are ultimately unachievable. Beauty is not objective, but socially and culturally determined, as evidenced by the wide-ranging ideas about beauty found across history and geography. Dominant beauty norms reinforce white supremacy. Those in the West – which influence the rest of the planet through media and advertising – are premised in ethnically European features, including eye and hair colour, hair texture, skin tone, bone structure and fat distribution. Feminists argue that the beauty myth serves to buttress existing social hierarchies, destroy womens' and girls' self-worth, and generate profits for beauty-based industries.

Feminism and femininity

Since the 1960s, feminists have challenged society's expectations that women be feminine. At the 1968 Miss America protest in Atlantic City, New Jersey, hundreds of feminists threw symbols of what they considered women's oppression into a 'Freedom Trash Can', resulting in the erroneous enduring stereotype of feminists as 'bra burners'. Susan Brownmiller, in her 1984 book *Femininity*, critiqued femininity as a 'nostalgic tradition of imposed limitations'. In 1990, feminist theorist Sandra Lee Bartky suggested that women police themselves to be appropriately feminine.

Many feminists have challenged these ideas about femininity, separating out coercive ideals from those that women embody out of joy, self-love and desire. Swedish feminist academic Ulrika Dahl writes about queer femme women who embody femininity not because they're working towards a male-defined ideal – indeed, many queer femme women don't even date men – but for pure pleasure, redefining what it means to be feminine.

Swedish self-proclaimed 'femme-inist' Ulrika Dahl in 2014.

Feminist masculinity

An important part of feminism involves analyzing how oppressive gender norms aren't just oppressive to women – they also limit the full emotional and creative expression of men. Proponents of feminist masculinity seek to cultivate masculinity that is based on self-love and respect for difference rather than on the rejection and shaming of femininity and dispensing brute power over others.

Black feminist theorist bell hooks wrote about feminist masculinity in her 2000 book *Feminism is for Everybody*, declaring, 'Boys need healthy self-esteem. They need love. And a wise and loving feminist politics can provide the only foundation . . . Patriarchy will not heal them. If that were so they would all be well.' Sociologist Michael Kimmel has championed similar notions in his books. Organizations, such as the US-based Good Men Project, founded in 2009, strive to provide positive outlets for men to share their struggles with each other and examine the meaning of manhood.

Postcolonial feminism

Many Western feminists mistakenly assume that women in the Global South are passive victims of patriarchy who need Western intervention. This assumption fails to account for women's movements in countries outside the West and assumes a Western framework for understanding what feminism can look like across different cultures and geographies.

Indian-American postcolonial feminist scholar Chandra Talpade Mohanty tackled this issue in her 1984 article 'Under Western Eyes'. She critiqued how Western feminists had created a homogenized idea of the helpless 'Third World woman', as if women in the Global South don't have diverse experiences, perspectives and forms of resistance to oppression. Similarly, Indian feminist scholar Gayatri Chakravorty Spivak, in her 1988 essay 'Can the Subaltern Speak?', chastized white Western women who believed they must 'sav[e] the brown women from brown men'. In contrast, postcolonial feminism centres the voices of women in the Global South and follows their lead in activism.

Women of the Iranian Green Movement protest in 2009 during the aftermath of Iran's presidential election.

Feminism and disability

The field of feminist disability studies seeks to incorporate perspectives on disability into feminism and vice versa. One important aspect of the intersection between disability activism and feminism is the fight for bodily autonomy.

Historically, women's bodies have been viewed as biologically deficient compared to those of men, while people with disabilities have been deemed incapable, stupid and in need of being treated like children. There has always been much overlap between issues of justice for women and people with disabilities.

Disability activists, as well as scholars of feminist disability studies, work towards shifting society's focus from pitying people with disabilities to making public policy and adapting the built environment to accommodate their needs. They argue, for example, that autism should not be seen as a 'problem', but as the failure of society to establish inclusive environments for neurodivergent people.

As the first Asian woman to be elected to US Congress in Illinois, as well as the first disabled woman elected to Congress, Tammy Duckworth has built a reputation on behalf of both women's and disability rights.

Postfeminism

A common way of rebutting the existence of feminism is to claim that society doesn't need it and that women and men are already equal. Such a response is 'postfeminist', a concept that emerged in the 1980s and early 1990s in the West as part of the conservative backlash against the progressive social movement gains of the 1960s and 1970s. Susan Bolotin used the term 'postfeminist' in a 1982 article published in *The New York Times* to refer to young women who aligned with feminist values but who declined to identify as feminist, showing that many women have internalized postfeminist ideology.

Cultural theorist Angela McRobbie argues that, in consuming porn, participating in hookup culture and reclaiming words like 'slut' and 'bitch', younger women risk becoming a 'postfeminist' generation by buying into their own misogynist subordination. However, the resurgence of feminism among young women in the 2000s and 2010s offers much evidence to counter concerns about a postfeminist generation.

SAME SHIT, DIFFERENT CENTURY

Women participate in a Time's Up rally, held in London in 2018. Feminists argue that as long as a society continues to be patriarchal, it can't be truly 'postfeminist'.

VOTES FOR WOMEN

First-wave feminism

Feminism in the 19th and early 20th centuries – later called the 'first wave' – primarily focused on the fight for suffrage, the right to vote. Most women supporting the cause belonged to the 'suffragist' branch of the movement, which focused on peaceful campaigning.

In contrast, the 'suffragettes', founded by British feminist Emmeline Pankhurst, were more radical and militant. They engaged in direct-action protests, such as confronting officials, chaining themselves to buildings, destroying property and going on hunger strikes in prison, which were met by force-feeding.

Another first-wave movement was the women's temperance movement. These women used moral arguments to advocate for the prohibition of alcohol. They argued that men, morally inferior to women, damaged the home through their consumption of alcohol, especially as it inspired them to commit violence and fritter money away.

Members of the Australian Women's Christian Temperance Union in 1918, including Union president Lady Julia Maria Holder.

Anarcha feminism

Anarcha feminists combine anarchist political theory with feminism, resulting in a movement that radically rejects political hierarchy and understands state-based violence as an expression of patriarchy that must be destroyed. In 'Who We Are: An Anarcho-Feminist Manifesto' (1971), Chicago anarcha feminists Black Maria and Red Rosia argued against '[the] rule by gangs of armed males calling themselves governments'.

Anarcha and socialist feminists have been active in anti-fascist and anti-authoritarian movements around the world since the early 20th century. The movement's roots can be traced to at least the 1800s through the writing and activism of Russian-US activist Emma Goldman, known as the mother of modern anarchism. Goldman attacked the patriarchal family, religion, repressive morality and the state as sites of women's oppression. She chose not to support the suffrage movement because she thought it would only help the most privileged women, instead fighting for birth control and free love.

Emma Goldman

Socialist feminism

Socialist feminism arose in the 1960s and 1970s. Organized by women invigorated by feminism and the ideas of the New Left, socialist feminists centre both capitalism and patriarchy in their political analysis. They focus on women's economic oppression, viewing the abuses of capitalism through a gendered lens and women's issues through a socialist lens. Most socialist feminists draw on the work of German socialist philosopher Karl Marx, reconfiguring many of his ideas to apply to women. Unlike Marx, who focused on fighting class oppression and believed gender oppression would cease as a result, socialist feminists such as British scholar Sheila Rowbotham argue that class oppression and gender oppression must be fought equally and in tandem. They argue that liberation for women under capitalism isn't possible; instead, a complete transformation of society on behalf of the worker is needed. Socialist feminists tend not to practise gender-based separatism, finding it important for men and women to work together for all people oppressed under capitalism.

Above, the NYC International Women's Strike. The term 'socialist feminism' is believed to have been first used in the 1972 manifesto of a chapter of the Chicago Women's Liberation Union.

Second-wave feminism

Second-wave, or 'liberal', feminism, can be understood as the most mainstream 'face' of modern Western feminism. It focuses on equality between the sexes, including pay equity, access to abortion and childcare and the representation of women in government and other professions. In contrast to other branches of feminism, such as anarcha and socialist feminism, it focuses on achieving legal and political reform from within dominant institutions rather than toppling those systems. Philosophically, liberal feminism aligns with classical liberalism in its focus on individual liberty and rights.

Disillusionment with the centring of white, middle- to upper-class, heterosexual women's issues in liberal feminist groups during the 1960s and 1970s helped drive the evolution of diverse movements, such as black feminism and radical lesbian feminism. Today, tensions between feminists as to whether they should promote reform or revolution continues to animate debates among the members of different groups.

Radical feminism

Emerging during the 1960s, radical feminism viewed men as the oppressor class and women as the victims of that oppression. In her 1969 manifesto 'Radical Feminism', Ti-Grace Atkinson wrote that women's oppression historically stemmed from men taking advantage of women's bodily vulnerability during pregnancy and childbirth. Radical feminists place special emphasis on men's sexual objectification of, and violence towards, women. During the movement's heyday in the 1970s and 1980s, famous radical feminists such as Gail Dines, Andrea Dworkin and Catharine MacKinnon were known for taking strong stances against sex work, porn and BDSM. Radical feminists were also instrumental in establishing women's refuges and rape crisis centres in the 1970s.

The cultural feminism of the 1970s, which holds that men and women have fundamentally different characteristics, was strongly influenced by radical feminism. Both schools seek a utopian future where 'women's' values of peace and nurturing triumph over 'men's' values of war and aggression.

The Venus symbol combined with the raised 'power' fist is often associated with radical feminism.

Trans-exclusionary radical feminism

Trans-exclusionary radical feminism (TERF) constitutes a sub-movement of radical feminism active since the 1970s. TERFs express vocal discomfort with transgender women, arguing that they aren't 'real' women at all, and are a threat to lesbian and all-women spaces. In 1979, Janice Raymond argued in *The Transsexual Empire: The Making of the She-Male* that all 'transsexuals rape women's bodies by reducing the real female form to an artefact, appropriating this body for themselves'. Some trans-exclusionary radical feminists (TERFs) 'dox' trans women by revealing their private information online and 'outing' them to their employers.

Trans-inclusive feminists argue that TERFs' harassment only bolsters the high murder rate of low-income trans women of colour in the United States, Brazil and other countries. Further, they argue, reducing trans women to their bodies is anti-feminist given feminists' long struggle towards being seen as complex subjects versus inferior bodies.

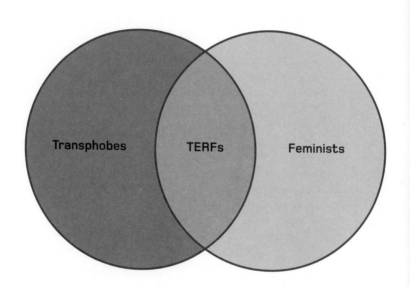

Ecofeminism

Ecofeminism, coined in 1974 by French feminist writer Françoise d'Eaubonne, is a branch of feminism connecting women's rights to environmentalism, viewing women and the planet as sacred life-bearers. It argues that patriarchy is the cause of the abuse of both women and nature.

Some ecofeminists centre spirituality, emphasizing the need to view the Earth as alive and all beings as interconnected. Many ecofeminists are staunch supporters of vegetarianism, veganism and animal liberation, challenging the notion that humans should be afforded more compassion and dignity than other living beings. They also argue that it was the rise of patriarchal religions that facilitated the worldview that nature is sinful or 'fallen', instead of divine, and that women are inferior to men.

Other ecofeminists focus on the material structures behind the destruction of both nature and women, such as labour exploitation and land theft.

Ecofeminists celebrate both women and the Earth, many arguing that the two share a sacred bond.

French feminism

French feminism refers to key texts written by French-speaking feminist theorists such as Hélène Cixous, Luce Irigaray and Julia Kristeva, from the 1970s to the 1990s. Highly abstract, the texts depart from the political pragmatism of most anglophonic feminism produced during the same period, immersed as they are in the theories of poststructuralism and psychoanalysis. French feminists critique how men have shaped philosophical knowledge while claiming to be 'objective' and universal.

The idea of sexual difference is central here, and suggests that women's unique ways of being and communicating have been stifled by men in literature, in the same way that men have stifled women's sexuality. To remedy this tendency, Cixous offered the theory of *écriture féminine* (feminine writing), encouraging women to write outside the 'rational' model sanctioned by men. Similarly, Irigaray asked women to lean into what makes them 'different' from men, such as their body's 'unruly' menstrual and breast milk fluids, and celebrate that difference through 'fluid' writing.

French feminist icon
Hélène Cixous

Black feminism

Black feminism developed in the United States, as a sanctuary for black women experiencing racism in the white-dominated women's movement and sexism in the male-dominated civil rights movement. Black feminist thinkers such as Audre Lorde, Angela Davis, bell hooks and Barbara Smith wrote about how black women's experiences are different from those of white women, starting from the days of slavery, when large numbers of white women engaged in, or were complicit with, black women's enslavement. Angela Davis, in her 1983 book *Women, Race, & Class*, explored the history of racism and classism that shaped white-dominated feminism. She analyzed how black women's womanhood has been treated very differently from that of white women in a racist society, how white women have betrayed black women's trust in the fight for gender equality, and how black women have faced different types of attack on their reproductive liberty than have white women. Davis, along with other black feminists, challenged what counted as 'women's issues', illustrating that black women's issues are inherently women's issues.

US Black feminist icon Angela Davis

Womanism

Conceptualized by US feminist writer, poet and activist Alice Walker in her 1983 book *In Search of Our Mothers' Gardens: Womanist Prose*, womanism explores womanhood from the perspective of black women. A celebration of black women's culture and spirituality, womanism was intentionally configured to avoid the label 'feminist' due to the ways that feminism has been, and often remains, dominated by white women and their interests to the exclusion and detriment of black women.

In the late 1980s, US scholar Clenora Hudson-Weems created the term 'Africana womanism', which celebrates African women who have contributed to womanism. It elevates concerns about racism and classism above those about sexism for a number of reasons, including the fact that relationships between black men and women are very different from that of white men and women. Further, from slavery onward, black families were forced into nontraditional gender roles; thus, according to Hudson-Weems, feminist critiques of patriarchal gender roles don't apply in the same way to black people in the United States.

The first Black Womanhood Conference at Connecticut College, USA in 1969.

Xicanisma

Xicanisma, also known as Chicana feminism, is a movement in the United States that focuses on the experiences of Chicana women. It was formed in the 1960s by women who had typically experienced sexism within the Chicano civil rights movement and racism within white-dominated feminist movements. Foundational to xicanisma is an embracing of Chicanas' cultural roots and female power in the face of white supremacy and imperialism.

Gloria Anzaldúa, a major figure in Chicana feminism, critiqued the misogyny and homophobia found within traditional Mexican culture, especially the idea that to be a 'good' woman, one had to be a (heterosexual) wife and mother. She also commented on the toxic masculinity known as 'machismo' in Mexican culture, condemning it, but also noting its roots in the shaming of Mexican men through historical conquest and racism. Equally important to Anzaldúa was cultivating self-love and honouring Mexican-American culture through a process of decolonization, which she often wrote about using poetic and spiritual frameworks.

Detail from a
Chicano mural at
Centro Cultural
de la Raza, Balboa Park,
San Diego, California.

Indigenous feminism

Indigenous feminism centres on native women in settler colonial societies, namely the United States, Canada, New Zealand and Australia. Supporters fight back against the intersections between misogyny, white supremacy, colonization, imperialism, genocide, sexual violence and forced sterilization as they impact indigenous women and tribal communities as a whole. They also challenge misogynist and homophobic ideas about gender and sexuality, which, they argue, came from European colonizers and were forced onto their communities. The development of modern indigenous feminism began in the 1970s. Many Native American women participated in the American Indian Movement (AIM) formed in 1968, which fought for tribal nations' economic independence. After women experienced sexism in AIM and a lack of attention to issues disproportionately impacting them, they formed their own groups, such as Women of All Red Nations (1974). Indigenous feminists are among the most cutting-edge community change makers of the 21st century as they fight for gender, racial and environmental justice across the globe.

A key component of indigenous feminism is honouring indigenous women's leadership roles within their traditional, matrilineal cultures.

Third World, postcolonial and transnational feminism

Feminists across the Global South continue to resist the patronizing, culturally insensitive and racist assumptions by Western feminists about their lives. In the 1980s, women began reclaiming the term 'Third World' – a term created by Europeans and North Americans to refer to 'underdeveloped' countries. Third World feminists promote grassroots women's rights activism and protest globalization's negative impacts on women, especially impoverishment and violence. They also critique Western military intervention and the imposition of Western beauty norms onto women in the Global South.

Postcolonial feminism shares many concerns with Third World feminism, but rejects the reclaiming of 'Third World', emphasizing the long-term impacts of colonialism in societies formerly occupied by colonial governments. Transnational feminism, meanwhile, focuses on capitalism, globalization, and the migration of people and ideas, choosing not to continue centring colonialism.

Nigerian feminist Chimamanda Ngozi Adichie
on the cover of *Ms.* magazine in 2014.

Islamic and Muslim feminism

Islamic and Muslim feminism both use Quranic teachings, as well as non-Muslim feminist ideas, to advocate for gender equality. Islamic feminists focus more exclusively on Islamic teachings and Muslim feminists draw more on outside secular sources. Both schools critique the patriarchal interpretations of the Qur'an, the hadith (sayings attributed to the prophet Muhammad) and sharia law, arguing that the Qur'an and hadith contain many lessons of equality. In 1992, Egyptian-American Leila Ahmed's book *Women and Gender in Islam* became a classic text for both schools.

A key area of activism is the reform of Muslim family law, specifically laws governing men's marriage to multiple wives, divorce, child custody and property. Rigid gender roles within the family are another area of protest, specifically the cloistering of women inside the home. These feminists also challenge compulsory dress codes, whether they be the forced wearing of burqas and abayas in Afghanistan and Saudi Arabia, or the complete ban of headscarves in public, as in France and Turkey.

Egyptian women protest sexual harassment in a 2013 march on Tahrir Square, Cairo, in the aftermath of the 2011 Egyptian Revolution of Dignity.

Third-wave feminism: intersectionality

Third-wave, or intersectional, feminism arose from the failure of many feminist movements of the 1960s and 1970s to be fully responsive to the needs of women of colour and poor and working-class women. Coined in 1991 by US black feminist legal scholar Kimberlé Crenshaw (see also, page 22), and building on women of colour feminist scholarship, the theory holds that women are more than their gender. They may also face racism, classism and other forms of oppression. For example, a black lesbian woman doesn't merely experience racism, sexism and homophobia, but homophobia that is racialized, racism that is sexualized, and so on. Analyzing Los Angeles-area women's shelters, Crenshaw wrote that even institutions intending to be pro-woman often end up reproducing the interests of those oppressed only by gender. The shelters she analyzed were often located in areas inaccessible via public transit, for example, with materials only in English. Intersectional feminism, in contrast, is about advocating for a feminism that uplifts the most marginalized women.

Postmodern feminism

Largely academic in approach, postmodern feminism applies the philosophical theory of postmodernism to gender. It includes both the French feminists (see page 58) as well as the widely-cited work of US philosopher Judith Butler. While intersectional feminists asked the question 'which women are we talking about?', postmodern feminism questions the very idea of what 'woman' means.

In 1990, Butler published *Gender Trouble*, in which she argued that, far from being based in biological truths, gender is determined by societal norms. According to her theory of gender performativity, people 'perform' their gender in daily tasks that effectively create their masculinity or femininity; for example, putting on lipstick or shaving one's facial hair into a goatee. These rituals must be constantly maintained to perpetuate the illusion that our gender is natural and stable. At any time, argued Butler, we could break away and perform our gender differently, exposing how gender is socially contingent and fluid.

US postmodern feminist philosopher Judith Butler

Trans feminism

Trans feminism focuses on the experiences of transgender communities, and fights for trans people's right to be treated with respect, both in a transphobic society and within feminist movements that remain exclusionary and hostile. Trans feminists question the systems of power that set rigid rules about the gender binary, including the medical field and prisons, which have dehumanized trans people and withheld life-saving resources. As an activist and intellectual movement, trans feminism began during the 1990s, with Sandy Stone's 1991 article 'The Empire Strikes Back', written as a rebuttal to virulently anti-trans arguments published by Janice Raymond in 1979. Kate Bornstein's 1994 book *Gender Outlaw* was crucial in exploding assumptions about maleness and femaleness. In 2001, Emi Koyama wrote 'The Transfeminist Manifesto', which popularized the term trans feminism and analyzed how race and class are as important in trans women's lives as gender. Julia Serano's 2007 book *Whipping Girl* analyzes cisgender feminists' transmisogyny as it connects to the rejection of femininity (femmephobia).

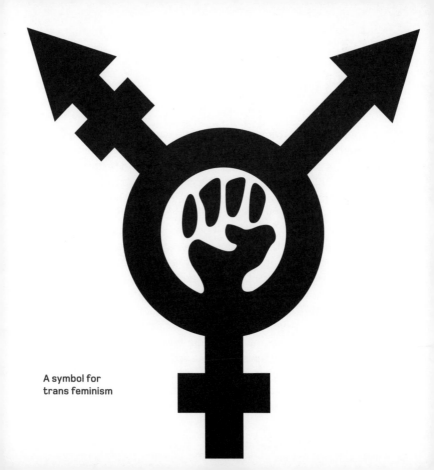

A symbol for
trans feminism

Fat liberation and body-positive feminism

Fat liberationists want to reclaim the word 'fat' from its stigmatizing and dehumanizing associations with being dirty, lazy, out of control, inherently unhealthy and immoral. They argue that fat people have the right to be loved and treated with respect rather than belittled, harassed and talked down to. Similarly, contemporary body-positive feminists believe in the inherent value of all bodies, regardless of size. In the 1960s, during the era of super-thin English model Twiggy, feminists joined with fat liberation activists to challenge how extreme thinness was being pushed as the ideal for women. In 1972, the group Fat Underground was formed in the United States, and in 1978, British psychoanalyst Susie Orbach wrote her pioneering anti-diet book *Fat is a Feminist Issue*. Today, fat-positive feminists want to change how society views fat women, pointing to studies showing that women of size earn less, are given fewer raises, and experience worse medical care as a result of doctors assuming ailments are weight-related without performing diagnostic checks.

Fourth-wave feminism

Feminism constituting a 'fourth wave' is, according to US feminist author Jennifer Baumgardner, traceable to 2008, when Western feminists began building a serious online presence through the feminist blogosphere. Driven mostly by younger generations who grew up with 'girl power' and the gains of feminism, fourth-wave feminism emphasizes intersectionality and sex positivity. Feminists of the fourth wave tend to feel that complete gender equity should be a given. Fourth-wave feminism is aided by access to online tools, such as inviting people to protests via Facebook, livestreaming rallies and taking to Twitter to share up-to-the-minute news on pending legislation and civil unrest. Prominent blogs and websites that helped inaugurate the fourth wave include Feministing, founded in 2004, and the 2005 anti-street harassment platform Hollaback!, created in New York to allow women to upload photos of their harassers. The global #MeToo movement against sexual harassment and assault is just the latest use of 'hashtag activism' by the fourth wave.

Fourth-wave feminists at a 2017 International Women's Day rally in London.

Pre-contact North America

Prior to the European invasion of what is now North America, indigenous tribes lived on the land for at least 10,000 years. Many of their societies were matrilineal, meaning that tribal members were identified through their mother's ancestral line. Women in these societies tended to hold important leadership roles. They also usually owned the family housing and goods. This gender equality was viewed as confounding and alien to the patriarchal European settlers who made contact with them.

Among the tribes of the matrilineal Iroquois Confederation (found in what are now the northeastern United States and southeastern Canada), while the chiefs were male, they were selected by female clan elders who also had the power to depose the chiefs and veto their decisions. When a man and woman joined together to create a family, the man would move in to the longhouse belonging to his wife's family. Their children became members of their mother's clan, and if their mother and father parted ways, the mother retained custody of her children.

Unlike white European women, indigenous women in pre-contact North America had considerably more respect and rights.

The Rights of Woman

Two 18th-century authors of recognizably feminist political texts were French playwright Olympe de Gouges and English philosopher Mary Wollstonecraft. Both wrote about the need for their societies to treat women as equal citizens. Active in a variety of political causes, de Gouges published a pamphlet in 1791 titled 'Declaration of the Rights of Woman and of the (Female) Citizen', in response to the Declaration of the Rights of Man and of the Citizen adopted in 1789 by the revolutionary National Assembly at the start of the French Revolution. Women, de Gouges asserted, were entitled to the same rights as men, and children born outside of marriage should be given the same inheritance rights as 'legitimate' children. The next year, in 1792, Wollstonecraft published her book *A Vindication of the Rights of Woman*, which argued that women should be educated equally to men. Educating women, she wrote, would not only prepare them as workers, but would also strengthen their roles as wives and mothers, thus positively impacting everyone in society.

Engraving of Mary Wollstonecraft c. 1797.

Marital rape

English jurist Sir Matthew Hale ruled in 1736 that marital rape didn't exist as a crime. According to Hale, this was because women automatically gave their husbands lifelong consent to sex through entering into marriage. In the 19th century, feminists such as Harriet Taylor and John Stuart Mill in England, as well as US suffragists Elizabeth Cady Stanton, Lucy Stone and Victoria Woodhull, challenged this view.

Hale's denial of women's bodily autonomy and his male-centred definition of marriage impacted English-speaking countries for centuries. It wasn't until 1991 that the United Kingdom, after decades of feminist activism, made marital rape illegal. In the United States, marital rape became illegal in all 50 states by 1993; yet even then, in only 17 states were marital and non-marital rape treated the same under the law. The United Nations High Commissioner for Human Rights established marital rape as a violation of international human rights in December 1993, but it continues to remain a problem worldwide.

Edgar Dégas, *Intérieur* (*Interior*) or *Le viol* (*The Rape*), c. 1868 to 1869.

Widow-burning in India

Practised since approximately 320 to 550 CE in India, Nepal and other parts of Hindu Southeast Asia, *sati*, also spelled *suttee*, is the practice of a widow burning herself alive on her husband's funeral pyre as an ultimate act of wifely devotion. Hindu women have historically faced social pressure to perform *sati*, especially women with no children and who would face a lifetime of poverty without their husbands. In some cases, women have been thrown onto pyres against their will, or buried alive in their husband's graves.

Leaders as far back as Muslim emperor Akbar the Great (c. 1500) have tried to ban *sati* over the centuries. The British, who banned the practice in 1829, stated at the time that prohibiting *sati* was the starting point for their 'civilizing mission' in the country. This is an important reminder for how Western claims about 'saving' women have often helped justify imperialism. Indian parliament passed an even stricter law against *sati* in 1988, and in the 21st century, the practice is almost non-existent.

'*Sati* hands – tragedy in stone' at the Mehrangarh
fort in Jodhpur, Rajasthan, India.

Enslavement in the United States

Under US slavery, black women were expected to perform the same labour as enslaved black men while also raising their children. During this time of terror and violence, black women didn't have the luxury of being viewed as human beings, let alone as sympathy-inducing mothers.

Narratives exist of enslavers whipping black women while they were pregnant. They forced the women to dig small holes in the ground and place their stomachs in them when lying down for their whippings, in order to protect the enslavers' foetal 'property'. As wet nurses to white women's babies, black women were often forced to leave their own babies hungry. Their families could be ripped apart at any time, their marriages denied recognition and their family members sold away. Rape by their enslavers and forced 'breeding' with enslaved men acted as the backdrop to their misery. Enslavers' wives, meanwhile, took out their jealousy and anguish over their cheating, sexually predatory husbands by further punishing the enslaved women.

An illustration from *Harper's Weekly*, 1867.

The Seneca Falls Convention

Held from 19th to 20th July 1848, in Seneca Falls, New York, the Seneca Falls Convention was the first women's rights convention in the United States. It was organized by Elizabeth Cady Stanton, Lucretia Mott, Martha Coffin Wright, Mary M'Clintock and Jane Hunt, all of whom were also involved in the abolitionist movement. Stanton and Mott had met at the 1840 World Anti-Slavery Convention in London and, after being excluded from full participation due to their gender, decided to create a convention for women's rights. Seneca Falls is considered the catalyst for the US women's suffrage movement.

Three hundred people attended the convention. The first day was devoted to women's speeches. On the second day men also spoke, including famous black civil rights leader Frederick Douglass, who spoke passionately in favour of women's suffrage. The convention's manifesto was called the 'Declaration of Sentiments'. Written mostly by Stanton, it argued, 'We hold these truths to be self-evident: that all men and women are created equal.'

In 1849, this satirical cartoon by George Cruikshank, rich with symbolism, served as backlash to the Seneca Falls Convention. Mocking women's femininity as unsuitable for leadership within a courtroom, it declared absurd a future in which women hold legal careers. For such nay-sayers, the rights women advocated for at Seneca Falls constituted a threat to women's 'place' as mothers in the domestic realm.

Matrimonial Causes Act of 1857

Passed by the UK parliament in 1857, the Matrimonial Causes Act was the first legislation to allow civil divorce, processed in a secular divorce court, rather than controlled by the Church of England. The act served as the foundation for later Matrimonial Causes Acts, the last in 1973, which together built the modern legal framework for divorce in the United Kingdom.

The new law also had an important social impact. As Victorian legal scholar Albert Venn Dicey wrote in 1905, '[The Act] in reality gave national sanction to the contractual view of marriage ... [and gave] strength to the belief that women ought, in the eye of the law, to stand substantially on an equality with men.' It is important to note, however, that under the act, while husbands could divorce based on proving a wife's adultery, women had to prove a husband's adultery in addition to cruelty or desertion, illustrating the continued societal double standards regarding gender, sexuality and power.

Prior to having the right to divorce their husbands, English women would sometimes be subjected to 'wife selling', in which their husbands sold them to the highest bidder. Originating in the late 17th century, the practice lingered until the early 20th century.

Victorian-era 'separate spheres'

The Industrial Revolution caused a shift in gender roles in Victorian-era Western Europe and North America. The transition from an agrarian economy to one driven by urban industry, as well as machines taking over work traditionally done by women, created a widening gulf between the unpaid maternal labour of the domestic realm and the male-dominated wage labour performed outside the home. In the process, Victorian society emphasized the idea of 'separate spheres', in which women's 'natural' province was the home, while men's was the public sphere of career and political participation. The ideal woman was implicitly white, middle- to upper-class, and possessed four key values: piety, purity, domesticity and submissiveness. Women, the men argued, were biologically suited for domesticity while being physically and emotionally ill-equipped for 'men's work'. In reality, many women departed from this model, including enslaved black women forced into a lifetime of hard labour, other women of colour, poor and working-class women and immigrant women.

George Elgar Hicks,
*The Sinews of
Old England*, 1857.

Feminism and the 'New Woman'

From the 1870s to the 1890s, writers such as Charles Reade, Sara Grand and Henry James began using the term 'New Woman' to refer to the growth of independent, educated women in Europe and North America. The New Woman was likely to be involved in the fight for women's suffrage and interested in sexual autonomy. Considered by dominant society to be frightening, unruly and usurping male authority, the New Woman was in control of her own life. As such, the concept was typically indicative of wealthy white women who had the financial means and racial privilege to achieve autonomy.

Unlike the idealized Victorian woman, the New Woman pushed against the social constraints that placed her firmly within the domestic sphere. She engaged in activities connecting her to the world outside the home, including working and bicycling. With increased access to higher education, as well as divorce laws, such women increasingly challenged the idea that their destiny was to become wives and mothers only.

A 1901 satirical photo titled 'New Woman – Wash Day'. The photograph mocks the concept of the New Woman and her supposedly inverted gender role, presenting her as inappropriately masculine while supervising her feminized husband as he performs the 'womanly' chore of doing laundry.

The Pankhursts and the suffragettes

The term 'suffragette' was first used in the UK to describe members of the Women's Social and Political Union (WSPU), the country's leading militant suffragist organization. Founded in 1903 by Emmeline Pankhurst, and true to its motto 'Deeds, not words', the WSPU tired of the moderate approaches organized by suffragists to date and sought radical action. The women destroyed property, heckled politicians, chained themselves outside parliament, interrupted meetings and organized mass demonstrations. Between 1908 and 1914, over 1,000 suffragettes were imprisoned, many of them staging hunger strikes to protest the UK government's refusal to classify them as political prisoners. In response, the jailers force-fed them, which amounted to torture. During World War I, the WSPU dissolved to focus on the war effort. Parliament would finally grant women over the age of 30 the right to vote in 1918, and in 1928 the vote became open to all women. The WSPU's actions inspired countless suffragists, including US suffragist Alice Paul, who founded the militant National Woman's Party.

Emmeline with her daughters Christabel and Sylvia Pankhurst in 1911. The WSPU became synonymous with the Pankhurst family name, illustrating that a wealthy married woman and her daughters could shake Britain to its core in transforming some of its most deeply held beliefs about women.

Emily Davison: martyr for women's suffrage

Born in London in 1872, English suffragette Emily Davison attended Royal Holloway College and Oxford University before joining the WSPU in 1906. Rejecting domesticity and prescribed gender roles, she eventually left her teaching job to devote herself to women's suffrage full time. Arrested on multiple occasions, she spent time in jail, where she was abused and, after going on hunger strikes, brutally force fed. On jumping off a jail balcony in 1912 she explained, 'I felt that by nothing but the sacrifice of human life would the nation be brought to realise the horrible torture our women face!'

In 1913, Davison ran onto the field at the Epsom Derby, possibly to drape a women's suffrage banner across one of the horses, before being hit and dying of her injuries. The queen mother demonized her as a 'brutal lunatic woman', while the press claimed her to be the 'first martyr' for women's suffrage. It has long been debated whether Davison intended to die that day. What is known is that she was a militant and steadfast champion for women's rights.

Davison's life work and ultimate sacrifice for the cause
of women's suffrage stand testimony to her refusal to play by
the narrow dictates constraining women during her lifetime.

Kartini schools, Indonesia

Raden Adjeng Kartini was an Indonesian advocate for girls' education and women's rights. Growing up in the 1880s and 1890s in an upperclass family in what was then the Dutch East Indies, Kartini learned about Western feminism by reading Dutch texts during her *pingit*, or period of seclusion before marriage. According to upperclass Javanese custom, from age 12 (when Kartini's formal education stopped) until their wedding day, girls weren't allowed to leave their parents' house.

Kartini became opposed to *pingit* as well as polygamy – her parents had pressured her into an arranged marriage with a man who had three wives. Kartini's dream of writing a book was cut tragically short in 1905 when she died in childbirth at age 25. However, in letters to pen pal Estella H. Zeehandelaar, Kartini discussed 'the impact of Dutch colonialism on gender and class, and ... the struggles of women of colour like her against the white colonizers.' Beginning in 1907, schools for girls called 'Kartini Schools' were opened across Indonesia.

In 1964, Kartini's birthday was declared
an Indonesian national holiday.

Feminist critiques of marriage

Russian-American anarchist Emma Goldman was critical of the impacts of (heterosexual) marriage on women. In her 1910 essay 'Marriage and Love', Goldman wrote, 'Marriage and love have nothing in common ... Marriage is primarily an economic arrangement, an insurance pact.' Marriage, argued Goldman, 'condemns [women] to life-long dependency, to parasitism, to complete uselessness, individual as well as social'. Instead, she advocated that women and men should be free to explore love and sex outside the rigid confines of marriage. Goldman's statements have been echoed by later feminists. Anthropologist Gayle Rubin wrote in 1975 that the history of Western marriage has largely been a history of men's economic exchange of women. Other feminists argue that as long as women continue to be paid less and forced to rely on men economically, marriage will remain a form of socially sanctioned prostitution. Still others question women taking their husband's last names, fathers 'giving away' their daughters on their wedding day, and other patriarchally-derived rituals.

Goldman with her lover Alexander Berkman, c. 1917 to 1919.
'Love' wrote Goldman, 'needs no protection: it is its own protection.'

1920s flappers flouting convention

The 'Roaring Twenties', as the 1920s are often called, were a time of economic prosperity, cultural innovation and changing roles for women. As women in multiple countries gained the right to vote, some politicians responded to the influx of new voters by focusing on issues that women tended to care about, including peace, education, and children. At the same time, the so-called 'Lost Generation' – people who came of age during World War I – had become jaded and cynical about the state of the world, and critical of the era's rampant materialism.

Young women labelled 'flappers' rebelled against the former constraints of the Victorian era. As minimum-wage laws and work reforms were passed, more women had money and time for entertainment. They abandoned corsets, adopted new fashions with shorter hemlines, bobbed their hair, engaged in drinking (formerly associated with men), wore cosmetics (long associated with sex workers), and listened to jazz in dance clubs. Female sexuality became less constricted, and in some circles, same-sex sexuality became more visible and normalized.

Eugenics and forced sterilization

In the late 19th and early 20th centuries, the eugenics movement arose as a way to control populations 'fit' for reproducing. Marginalized communities were deemed undesirable, especially communities of colour, people with disabilities, poor people and LGBTQ people. In the United States, black, Latina and Native American women became heavily targeted for forced sterilization programs, leading to a legacy of pain and distrust between those communities, the US government and the science and medical fields.

Under the watch of state eugenics boards, poor black women and girls were coerced into sterilizations or sterilized without their knowledge during other medical procedures. Indigenous, Puerto Rican and Latina immigrant women were similarly targeted. According to scholar Jane Lawrence, from 1970 to 1976, 25 to 50% of Native American girls and women were sterilized by the Indian Health Service, resulting in a decline in the fertility of Native Americans from 1970 to 1980.

The 'many sources' from which eugenics draws are various fields of human endeavour represented by the roots of the eugenics 'tree'.

Motherhood and authoritarianism

In World War II-era Stalinist Russia and Nazi Germany, the figure of the mother was used in government propaganda. Both regimes blended the sexist belief that women's highest calling should be motherhood with existing folk customs about the country as the 'motherland'. Just as the government served as 'mother' to the 'children' (citizens) of the country, so, too, was it women's duty to reproduce in service to the nation. Under Joseph Stalin, motherhood was emphasized as a patriotic duty, and women who had at least ten children were awarded the title of Mother Heroine. Russia's birth rate declined, however, as Stalin's rule pushed the country into poverty and starvation.

In Nazi Germany, blonde, blue-eyed mothers were championed as pivotal to securing the future for the 'master' Aryan race. To that end, the Nazis banned all forms of birth control and abortion for those deemed 'fit', created social programs and schools for mothers to further indoctrinate them and awarded women who produced many children with medals called the Mother's Cross.

The ideal German family in 1943, the boy proudly wearing his Hitler Youth uniform.

Simone de Beauvoir's
The Second Sex

French feminist philosopher Simone de Beauvoir published *The Second Sex* in 1949, serving as inspiration for women throughout the repressive 1950s and for the feminists of the 1960s, 1970s and beyond. In this book de Beauvoir asked, what is a woman? Under a patriarchal society, she argued, woman means man's 'other'; a human lacking maleness, and therefore man's inferior. De Beauvoir located women's inferior status in their bodily vulnerability during pregnancy and motherhood, writing that 'motherhood left woman riveted to her body like the animal.' *The Second Sex* is known for its early discussion of how society creates and shapes ideas about gender, as expressed through de Beauvoir's famous statement, 'One is not born, but rather becomes, a woman.' Another of de Beauvoir's major tasks in *The Second Sex* was to chart women's oppression throughout history. Her critique of psychoanalysis, and her theory of lesbian sexuality as a way to break away from patriarchal control, were additional ideas that put the book well ahead of its time and an influence on feminist theory for generations.

Betty Friedan: The 'problem that has no name'

In 1963, US feminist Betty Friedan published *The Feminine Mystique*, a landmark text for 1960s and 1970s feminism. The book was the product of Friedan being asked in 1957 to take a survey of her classmates from Smith College (a prestigious US women's college) for their 15-year anniversary reunion. Friedan found that, despite their education, many of her classmates expressed dissatisfaction with their post-college housewife lives. After interviewing other (white, heterosexual, class-privileged) suburban women, Friedan wrote about the 'problem that has no name': women's unhappiness, and shame about feeling unhappy, in response to being limited to the roles of wife and mother. She argued, radical at the time, that women's dissatisfaction wasn't a personal failing but rather a symptom of women's oppression in society. She challenged housewives' confinement to the domestic sphere, arguing that women should be just as free to pursue a career. Frieden went on to help found the National Organization for Women, serving as its first president in 1966.

French abortion rights

Written in 1971 by French feminist philosopher Simone de Beauvoir, the 'Manifesto of the 343' was a declaration in support of legal abortion in France, signed by 343 French women who had undergone abortions illegally. Published in *Le Nouvel Observateur* magazine, the manifesto declared that one million French women had abortions each year in dangerous conditions due to the procedure's illegality. The women who signed the manifesto were courageous: not only did they publicly reveal that they'd had abortions, but their signatures amounted to confessing to a crime for which they could be prosecuted. Opponents derided the document as the 'Manifesto of the 343 Sluts' and the 'Manifesto of the 343 Bitches', proving how misogyny is directly connected to the control of women's bodies and sexuality. French satirical paper *Charlie Hebdo* published sexist cartoons mocking the women. However, the women's bravery led to 331 French doctors signing their own manifesto on behalf of abortion rights. By January of 1975, abortion during the first 10 weeks of pregnancy was legalized across France.

Protest for abortion rights in 1970s Paris, France.

Abortion rights versus reproductive justice

Different groups of women have unique histories and priorities relating to reproduction and motherhood. While white Western women have had to fight for their right to curb their reproduction, women of colour, especially poor and working-class women of colour, have had to fight for the right to become mothers in the face of eugenics and forced sterilization campaigns. Many white supremacist and nativist movements have emphasized limiting the reproduction of communities of colour to preserve the dominance of the 'white race'.

In 1994, to reflect these concerns, US feminist activist and writer Loretta Ross helped coin the term 'reproductive justice' to link reproductive rights to a broader social justice framework. Reproductive justice includes the right to have children, not to have children and the ability to raise children in a safe and healthy environment. In pursuit of these goals, Ross co-founded the organization SisterSong Women of Color Reproductive Justice Collective in 1997.

Loretta J. Ross

Loretta Ross, co-founder of SisterSong Women of Color Reproductive Justice Collective, helped coin the term 'reproductive justice'.

The global fight for same-sex marriage

Same-sex marriage has occurred since ancient times, from the Roman emperor Nero entering into two publicly celebrated same-sex marriages with Pythagorus and Sporus, to 19th-century English noblewoman Anne Lister writing about her lover Mariana Belcombe, 'She is my wife in honour and in love and why not acknowledge her [as] such openly and at once?'

LGBTQ activists have long fought for legal same-sex marriage. The issue emerged as a life or death question during the 1980s AIDS crisis, when partners of those afflicted routinely found they had no control over medical or legal decisions due to not being legally married. The Netherlands became the first country to legalize same-sex marriage in 2000. In 2006, South Africa became the first to legalize it in Africa. By the end of the decade, ten countries on four continents had made it legal. In 2015, Ireland became the first country both to approve same-sex marriage via popular referendum and as a right enshrined under its constitution. Activists across the globe continue the fight.

A woman supports a same-sex marriage protest in Brisbane, Australia.

The 'lesbian baby boom'

In the United States during the 1990s, heightened visibility for gay and lesbian people, as well as developments in assisted reproductive technology, led increasing numbers of middle- to upper-class lesbian and bisexual women to have children. The trend emerged in the context of the ongoing right-wing US 'culture wars' against queer families, in which LGBTQ people were attacked by conservative politicians and religious figures as morally unfit for parenthood. In 1999, the American Civil Liberties Union published a report titled 'Overview of Lesbian and Gay Parenting, Adoption and Foster Care' refuting such arguments and using recent research to point to the positive life outcomes of children raised by same-sex parents.

Since the 1990s, same-sex parents have been having even more children, especially through adoption, despite the US continuing to lack federal adoption protections for LGBTQ families. According to the Williams Institute at UCLA, same-sex couple households were raising almost 220,000 children under the age of 18 in 2013.

A lesbian couple with their children, as featured in a photography exhibition showcasing CIA officers' thoughts on family, diversity and inclusion.

Public breastfeeding as a feminist issue

Breastfeeding is a basic life function that women have done throughout human history. In patriarchal societies that sexualize women's bodies, however, breastfeeding, especially in public, has become taboo. Women are often under extreme social pressure to avoid breastfeeding in front of others.

In the West, according to food studies scholar Amy Bentley, public stigma against breastfeeding increased after World War II, when breasts began to be highly sexualized in Hollywood. The more they became associated with sex, the more their connection to feeding children became culturally unsavoury. Then, as fewer Western white women breastfed publicly while women in the 'Third World' continued to do so, public breastfeeding also came to be viewed as 'uncivilized' within a racist worldview. Many feminists, meanwhile, argue that women should be able to breastfeed whenever they need to instead of being forced to duck into a dirty public bathroom or spend extra money on formula and breast pumps.

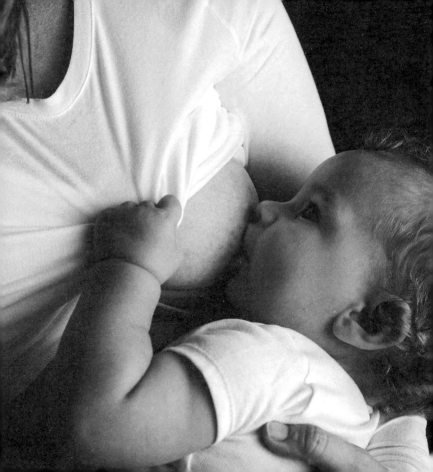

Polish abortion rights: the 'Black Monday' strike

On 'Black Monday', 3rd October 2016, thousands of women in over 60 Polish cities – and in other European cities such as London, Brussels and Berlin – left work in a nationwide strike. They donned black and took to the streets, protesting legislation that would further strip them of their abortion rights. Poland's abortion law is already one of the most restrictive in Europe: it is illegal except when the woman's life is in danger, the foetus is irreparably damaged or the pregnancy is the product of rape or incest. Under the new legislation, all abortions would have been banned, and women who sought one, along with their doctors, would face up to five years in prison.

Protesters in Warsaw blocked the entrance to the central government building, chanting, 'We want doctors, not missionaries!', referring to the Catholic church's support of the abortion ban. Three days later, Poland's parliament voted against the measure 352 to 58, illustrating the power of the Black Monday strike.

A young woman in support of the Black Monday protest against anti-abortion law in Poland, October 2016.

Together for Yes: Irish abortion rights victory

Abortion was first banned in Ireland in 1861. Almost a century later, in 1983, an additional act was passed – the Eighth Amendment – giving foetuses equal rights with women. Anti-choice activists had lobbied for this fearing abortion could become legal should the law be overturned., and the act was passed following a voters' referendum.

Then, in 2012, Savita Halappanavar entered an emergency room in Galway, Ireland, suffering an extended miscarriage. Because the staff continued to find a foetal heartbeat, her requests for an abortion were denied, even as she began entering septic shock. After several days, Halappanavar died from a sepsis-induced heart attack, galvanizing abortion rights advocates across the globe. In March 2018, Irish voters were finally allowed another referendum. The Together for Yes campaign led the victory to repeal the Eighth Amendment. The 'yes' voters gained a 66% majority, leading the Irish Oireachtas (parliament) to initiate the process of making abortions legal.

Together for Yes stickers and bouquets of flowers at a Dublin mural honouring Savita Halappanavar.

Women and peasant movements

In her 1998 book *Caliban and the Witch: Women, the Body, and Primitive Accumulation*, Italian-US feminist scholar Silvia Federici related the attacks on women during the European witch hunts to the transition from medieval feudalism to capitalism. She argued that capitalism was just one of many possible outcomes to replace feudalism and that its ascent was never guaranteed, as strange as that may seem to us now. Anti-feudal peasants' movements advocated for wealth-sharing, the rejection of hierarchies and sometimes sexual liberation. Federici identified women's involvement in these movements as 'the first evidence in European history of a grassroots women's movement'.

Far from being a hands-off, 'laissez-faire' system, capitalism was built on state violence. In stripping away women's power, terrorizing the population, and destroying communal solidarity via the witch hunts, peasants' resistance to the new proto-capitalist system could be quashed, while women's bodies and labour could be controlled.

Pieter Brueghel the Elder, *Spring*, 1565

The Women's March on Versailles

On the morning of 5th October 1789, the women of Paris had had enough of their families starving while the French monarchy lived in gilded opulence at Versailles. Bristling with rage at the scarcity and sky-high prices of bread, women gathered with makeshift weapons sourced from their kitchens. They joined together with some male revolutionaries and marched through the streets, the crowd surging into the thousands. After bursting into the city armoury and taking up arms, the women and their compatriots marched all the way to Versailles, where they violently stormed the palace and forced Louis XVI, Marie Antoinette, the couple's children and others in the court and the French Assembly to march to Paris with the crowd to face judgement. The Women's March was one of the first events of the French Revolution, occurring just a couple of months after the storming of the Bastille. In rising up against monarchical power and challenging the fate prepared for them based on their class and gender, these women remind us of female power in the face of deprivation and desperation.

An illustration of the Women's March on Versailles in
James Harvey Robinson's 1919 text *Medieval and Modern Times.*

Sheffield Female Political Association

The Sheffield Female Political Association was founded in the early industrial city of Sheffield, England, in 1851, as the UK's first organization for women's suffrage. Co-founder Anne Knight, a Quaker feminist and abolitionist, created the first known leaflet on women's suffrage, which was published in 1847. The women who formed the Sheffield group had been active participants in fighting for a six-point plan called the People's Charter as part of the working-class Chartist movement. The charter sought universal suffrage for men, higher wages for workers and other economic reforms to elevate the lives of poor and working-class Britons. Just as Chartists submitted petitions signed by millions of working-class people to the House of Commons, so too did the Sheffield Female Political Association submit a petition for women's suffrage to the House of Lords after gaining the support of the radical Earl of Carlisle. Their efforts illustrate that the history of women's suffrage in the UK extends beyond the realm of economically privileged women, with roots in the everyday struggles of working people.

Anne Knight in 1855. She holds a sign that reads,
'By tortured millions / By the divine redeemer /
Enfranchise Humanity / Bid the Outraged World / BE FREE'.

Jennie Collins, Bostonian class warrior

Working-class suffragist, labour activist and abolitionist Jennie Collins was born in New Hampshire, USA, in 1828. She took a passionate stand for women's labour rights based on her own experiences being orphaned as a child and working in cotton mills to support herself at the age of 14. While working as a domestic in Boston, she took night classes in history and politics. In 1868 Collins gave her first public speech on women's rights and spoke at the conference of the Daughters of St. Crispin, the first women's trade union in the United States.

Collins eventually became a well-known Boston speaker on labour and women's rights. She spoke out against child labour, women's starvation wages and poor working environments, and in favour of an eight-hour working day. In 1870, Collins founded a Boston centre for working and homeless women. Called Boffin's Bower, it was noteworthy for being founded by a woman from the same socioeconomic background as those she assisted.

John Hyde's depiction of Boffin's Bower, No. 1031 Washington Street, Boston, which appeared in *Frank Leslie's Illustrated Newspaper* in 1875.

Victoria Woodhull

In 1872, the Equal Rights Party put forth Victoria Woodhull as the first woman ever nominated for US president. Born in Ohio in 1838, Woodhull was a radical activist who founded and published *Woodhull & Claflin's Weekly* with her sister Tennessee Claflin. Woodhull's other notable accomplishments were becoming heavily involved in the spiritualist movement, opening the first female stock brokerage on Wall Street with Claflin, and becoming the first woman to address a US congressional committee when she lobbied for women's rights before the House Judiciary Committee.

Woodhull was known for her bold and, according to some, scandalous ideas. Her presidential platform included women's suffrage, an eight-hour workday, welfare for the poor, regulating monopolies, nationalizing the railroads and abolishing the death penalty. She also wrote in favour of legalizing sex work (although was not a fan of women exploited under it) and championed socialism, birth control and free love.

Victoria Woodhull c. 1860. On the topic of free love,
Woodhull wrote, 'I have an inalienable, constitutional and
natural right to love whom I may, to love as long
or as short a period as I can...'

The Irish Women Workers' Union

Founded in Dublin in 1911, the Irish Women Workers' Union (IWWU) was formed to provide female workers with access to a trade union after other trade unions discriminated against them based on their gender. Delia Larkin and Rosanna 'Rosie' Hackett helped found the IWWU. Fellow co-founder Constance Markievicz argued that forming a women's trade union would help women not only in the workplace, but also on the path to suffrage and better treatment in society overall. Professions the IWWU helped unionize included soup-kitchen workers, nurses, midwives, laundry workers, box makers and printers. By 1918, the IWWU had approximately 5,000 members. In 1945, the organization led a three-month strike that resulted in Irish women being granted the right to two weeks of paid holidays per year. The IWWU also helped secure court victories on behalf of female workers' fair treatment in the early 1980s. While it merged with the Federated Workers' Union of Ireland in 1984, the IWWU is remembered as pivotal in influencing both the male-dominated trade union movement and Irish government on behalf of women's labour rights.

IRISH
WOMEN

IW
WU

WORKERS
UNION

Members of the Irish Women Workers' Union on the steps of Liberty Hall, Dublin, c. 1914.

Triangle Shirtwaist Factory fire

On 25th March 1911, a fire broke out at the Triangle Shirtwaist Factory in Manhattan. The factory made women's shirts, known as 'shirtwaists', and employed young immigrants, mostly Italian and Jewish women between the ages of 14 and 23. Workers were paid hourly rates equal to $3.50-5.90 (£2.60–4.50) an hour today. The employers routinely locked the doors to prevent theft and to force the workers into productivity, so many exits were blocked. As a result, 146 workers died, many plunging to their deaths as they tried to escape the flames and smoke. The Triangle fire is important for feminism in that it spurred the passing of dozens of laws from 1911 to 1913 related to workers' safety, fire codes and restrictions on the hours women and children were allowed to work. The International Ladies' Garment Workers' Union grew in the aftermath. Unfortunately, the same issues connected to capitalist greed and the devaluation of poor women's labour continue to plague modern workers in the Global South, as evidenced by the lethal 2012 Tazreen Fashion factory fire in Dhaka, Bangladesh.

A demonstration of protest and mourning for Triangle Shirtwaist Factory Fire of 25th March 1911, was held on 5th April 1911.

Working-class suffragette Annie Kenney

One of 11 siblings, and employed at a cotton mill since the age of 10, English suffragette Annie Kenney was born into working-class toil. She had her finger ripped off during one of her 12-hour shifts at the mill, where she worked for 15 years. After she and her sister Jessie heard Christabel Pankhurst speak about women's rights in 1905, they became involved in the Women's Social and Political Union (WSPU), the leading UK militant women's suffrage organization from 1903 to 1917.

With Pankhurst, Kenney confronted Winston Churchill at a rally in 1905 to ask if the Liberal government would grant women's suffrage. Kenney was arrested and sent to prison 13 times for her activism, during which time she went on hunger strike. Kenney reportedly had an intimate relationship with Pankhurst, along with several other WSPU members. When Pankhurst fled to Paris in 1912 and installed Kenney as the head of the WSPU's London chapter, Kenney was the group's only working-class member to hold a leadership position.

Pictured (left) with Christabel Pankhurst, Annie Kenney released a memoir in 1924, *Memories of a Militant*.

East London Federation of Suffragettes

The East London Federation of Suffragettes (ELFS) was a radical group within the WSPU, established by Sylvia Pankhurst and Amy Bull in 1913. However, Pankhurst and Bull disagreed with the direction of the WSPU. They wanted a more democratic organization as well as an explicitly socialist one in order to advocate for working-class women's issues and the struggles of the working class in general.

Sylvia Pankhurst, who'd long had political tensions with her mother, WSPU founder Emmeline Pankhurst, was expelled from the union for these differences. In 1914, the ELFS emerged as its own organization. It lasted for ten years, fighting for equal pay, controls on food prices, a living wage and decent pensions. When World War I broke out, the ELFS took a position against the war while helping those most impacted by it. Its members organized the distribution of milk to starving babies, opened a children's health clinic staffed by volunteers and even founded their own toy factory to help stem unemployment while paying a living wage.

Contemporary mural in Bow, East London, by artist Jerome Davenport. It commemorated Sylvia Pankhurst and the East London Federation of Suffragettes.

Sekirankai and Japanese socialist feminism

Active in Japan in 1921, Sekirankai (Red Wave Society) was founded by several accomplished anarchist feminists, such as Yamakawa Kikue, who drafted the group's manifesto, and Ito Noe, active in Tokyo's feminist scene since 1913. Sekirankai's manifesto declared, 'The capitalist society turns us into slaves at home and oppresses us as wage slaves outside the home. It turns many of our sisters into prostitutes. Its imperialistic ambitions rob us of our beloved fathers, children, sweethearts and brothers and turns them into cannon fodder ... Socialism offers the only way to save mankind from the oppressions and abuses of capitalism. Sisters who love justice and morality, join the socialist movement!'

After participating in the 1921 May Day workers' march, members of Sekirankai were arrested. Noe and other revolutionaries were murdered by the secret police in 1923. Sekirankai dissolved in 1925, but a few members went on to form the socialist feminist group Yokakai (Eighth-Day Society).

Japanese anarchist and feminist Ito Noe, c. 1910 to 1923.

Frances Perkins' US labour leadership

The first US woman to hold a cabinet position, Frances Perkins served as the Secretary of Labor under President Franklin D. Roosevelt from 1933 to 1945. A former science teacher and social reformer, as Secretary of Labor, Perkins instituted the federal Social Security programme as well as the Fair Labor Standards Act, the former of which remains key in the meagre government safety net Americans rely on today.

Perkins' influence on Roosevelt's New Deal, which gave Americans profound economic relief from the Great Depression, cannot be overstated. In addition to creating Social Security to provide a modicum of economic security to the elderly, she convinced the president to initiate federal public works projects to create new jobs and to provide federal unemployment assistance. Other areas included regulating child labour, workers' wages and weekly hours worked. Despite being targeted by angry businessmen and facing right-wing attacks, Perkins was one of only two cabinet members to serve throughout Roosevelt's four terms in office.

Frances Perkins receiving a gold medal from Mrs Eleanor Roosevelt at the White House. Perkins was honoured as America's Outstanding Woman in the Field of Civic Achievement for 1934.

'We Can Do It!': female workers during WWII

The outbreak of World War II generated a mass exodus of men to fight on the front lines. As a result, many Western economies experienced a worker shortage. The US Office of War Information created campaigns urging women to enter the workforce patriotically on behalf of their men. Female workers were able to use this as an opportunity to break into many typically male-dominated fields hostile to women. In popular culture, the song 'Rosie the Riveter' became a hit, and Norman Rockwell created a painting titled *Rosie the Riveter* in 1943.

Women entered into the workplace in unprecedented numbers during this time. Between 1940 and 1945, the female share of the US workforce grew 10%, from 27% to nearly 37%. In 1943, 65% of the aviation industry workforce was female. By 1945, almost one in four married women worked outside the home. Women were paid far less than men for their work, however. At the end of the war, women were encouraged to return to the domestic realm and give men 'their' jobs back.

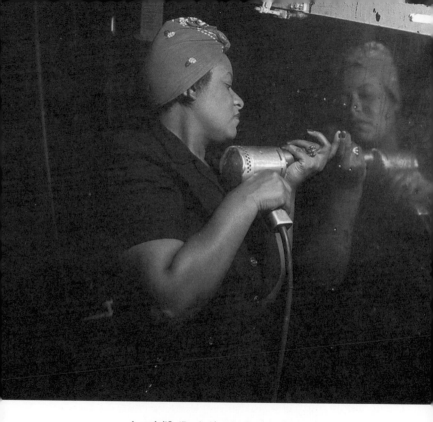

A real-life 'Rosie the riveter' works on an
A-31 Vengeance dive bomber in Tennessee, 1943.

Dolores Huerta and farm workers' rights

Working as a teacher in Stockton, California in the 1950s, New Mexico native Dolores Huerta turned to organizing farm workers after witnessing workers' children arriving at school hungry. After meeting labour activist César Chávez, the two co-founded the National Farm Workers Association

in 1962, followed by the United Farm Workers' Union in 1965. During the 1965 Delano strike, Huerta, while facing both sexism and racism, successfully organized 5,000 grape workers and secured their first union contract. She led a nationwide boycott of table grapes in the late 1960s that also resulted in a union contract, and she fought for workers' rights in the face of unsafe working conditions and exposure to toxic pesticides. Huerta's 1973 grape boycott led to the passage of the 1975 California Agricultural Labor Relations Act, which gave farm workers the right to form unions. US President Barack Obama honored her with the Presidential Medal of Freedom in 2012.

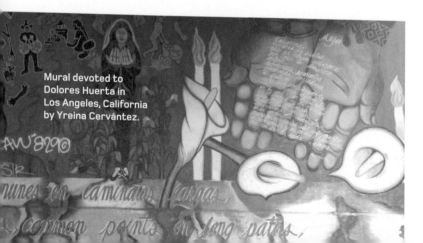

Mural devoted to Dolores Huerta in Los Angeles, California by Yreina Cervántez.

Ford machinists' strike in Dagenham

At the Ford Motor Company's plant in Dagenham, London, in 1968, female sewing machinists who made car seat covers learned that the company was downgrading their jobs from class C (skilled production) to class B (less skilled production). This meant a 15% cut in pay compared to their male colleagues performing similar tasks elsewhere in the factory. The women went on strike for four weeks, which led to the shutdown of the plant, until Ford agreed to pay them 92% of the wages given to men working under class B. They would not have their positions deemed class C again until 1984, when female workers launched a six-week strike.

The Dagenham workers' strike has had a lasting legacy. It inspired other female workers to form the National Joint Action Campaign Committee for Women's Equal Rights, which in 1969 held a demonstration in Trafalgar Square, London, for equal pay. It also directly led to the passage of the 1970 UK Equal Pay Act, which went into force in 1975, and in 2010 inspired the film *Made in Dagenham*.

The Ford sewing machinist women's strike acted as a springboard for the 1970 UK Equal Pay Act.

Li Xiaojiang: bringing women's studies to China

From 1966–1976, China's Great Proletarian Revolution resulted in the politics of radical class struggle dominating public conversation. Because of this emphasis on class, discussions of gender and sexuality were eclipsed. After leader Mao Zedong's death in 1976, women's rights advocates were able to shift the focus and identify women's place in society as a topic worthy of exploration. During this time, scholar Li Xiaojiang emerged as a leading voice for women's rights. She became known as the founder of women's studies in China.

Li was interested in talking about class struggle, but also how it applied to women's lives. She was critical of what she saw as the masculinization of women under Mao's rule, arguing that women should be able to remain feminine if they desire while also being considered equal to men. Of particular concern for Li was Chinese women's lives in the years after Mao's death. If China was experiencing a 'socialist era of gender equality', Li wrote, '[w]hy did women still feel so worn out and repressed?'

Chinese women and girls, argued Li, should be able to express femininity without being seen as inferior to men.

Socialist Filipina feminism

At the 2017 She For She forum, held in Manila, the Philippines, socialist feminist Senator Risa Hontiveros declared, 'The political language and value of our beloved country is still beset by a culture of misogyny.' As a socialist feminist, Hontiveros has been involved in a number of human rights and women's movements, emphasizing economic justice as it relates to women. A vocal critic of autocratic President Rodrigo Duterte's war on drugs, in which people accused of drug dealing have been executed by Duterte's vigilante death squads, Hontiveros has drawn attention to the impact of these executions on women. Many of the murdered men, Hontiveros has pointed out, have left behind wives and children who languish in dire poverty. Within the larger landscape of Filipina feminism, socialist feminist groups occupy an important place in fighting for women's rights. One such group is GABRIELA (General Assembly Binding Women for Reforms, Integrity, Equality, Leadership and Action). This national network of grassroots groups fights poverty, sex trafficking, rape culture, lack of health care, militarism and the negative impacts of globalization.

Risa Hontiveros at a 2010 Liberal Party campaign event in Antipolo City, the Philippines.

Naomi Klein and anti-capitalist feminism

Canadian writer and activist Naomi Klein is a leading voice of contemporary Western anti-capitalist feminism. In contrast to liberal feminists seeking equality between the sexes within the capitalist system, Klein rejects 'career feminism' and the emphasis on women's advancement in the corporate boardroom.

Klein explored the imposition of destructive capitalist policies in the aftermath of disasters and their disproportionate negative impacts on women and girls. She cited the rapid privatization of Iraq's economy, for example, after the US-led invasion of the country in 2003. She has written multiple articles critical of the Iraq War, arguing that US President George W. Bush orchestrated a capitalist restructuring of Iraq that benefitted outside investors and contractors rather than the Iraqi people. A committed environmentalist, Klein has also advocated that the US-based Occupy Wall Street movement join with the environmentalist movement to take down the corporate greed she argues is at the root of both movements' grievances.

Naomi Klein. Anti-capitalist feminists argue that feminism is a failed economic system that exploits the labour of all marginalized groups, including women.

Gendered labour under global capitalism

In 2012, just over 100 years after the Triangle Shirtwaist Factory fire in New York (see page 144), a fire broke out at the Tazreen Fashion factory near Dhaka, Bangladesh. At least 117 people were killed. As in the Triangle fire, most of the workers at Tazreen were young women, and employers had reportedly locked workers into the factory, contributing to the death toll. As a result, Bangladesh initiated new workplace safety standards. The factory produced apparel for many Western brands, and more than 100 European and US companies have since pledged to finance better upkeep in the Bangladeshi factories they contract with. The parallels between the Triangle and Tazreen fires point to how, as Western workers' rights have somewhat strengthened in the past century, the growth of global capitalism has meant that corporations simply turn to the Global South to find workers they can easily exploit for profit. Due to the feminization of poverty, women and girls in particular are impoverished and endangered globally in order to produce cheap goods for the West.

Abdul Jabbar, 26, holds his son Masum, 18 months, as he displays a photograph of his wife Mahfouza Kahtun, 22, a sewing-machine operator who died in the fire at Tazreen Fashions.

Occupy Wall Street

Forged in the aftermath of the 2008 financial crisis, the 2011 Occupy Wall Street movement against economic inequality unfolded first in Zuccotti Park, New York City. Marching by the thousands, protesters chanted, 'We are the 99%!' The slogan was an indictment of the top 1% of the economic elite, whose decadent luxury, protesters argued, came at the price of exploiting the labour of everyone else. The movement was critiqued for its alleged lack of diversity, unified message and tangible results; yet Occupy elevated income inequality as a national political issue and helped propel the campaign for a $15 minimum wage. Women were involved at all levels of the leaderless movement, from cooking and distributing food to strategizing in a women's working group. Footage of women being pepper-sprayed by police garnered Occupy its first mainstream media attention. At the same time, many female participants critiqued Occupy as being a haven for left-wing men who chose to focus myopically on class oppression rather than analyzing its connections also to sexism and racism.

Woman at Occupy Wall Street in New York City

WARNING: DO NOT CONFUSE THE COMPLEXITY OF THIS MOVEMENT WITH CHAOS

Ancient representations of female sexuality

Archaeologists, anthropologists and art historians have found frank representations of women's sexuality in numerous ancient cultures. The Indian text Kama Sutra (c. 400 BCE to 200 CE), for example, discusses the importance of female sexual pleasure, including the need for men to focus on eliciting women's orgasms. In Ireland, figurines named *sheela na gigs* depict naked women holding open their prominently-displayed vulvas with their hands. Theories as to the significance of these figurines include warding off evil and death, honouring a goddess and assisting in fertility. While no one truly knows their meaning, some modern feminists have suggested that *sheela na gigs* represent powerful contestations of misogyny. Art historian Tara Burk argues, 'Typical representations of the female nude in the European artistic tradition [from ancient Greece onwards] were made by male artists, who put woman on display for the pleasure of a presumed male spectator.' Thus, ancient representations of female sexuality do not necessarily indicate cultures committed to women's sexual liberation.

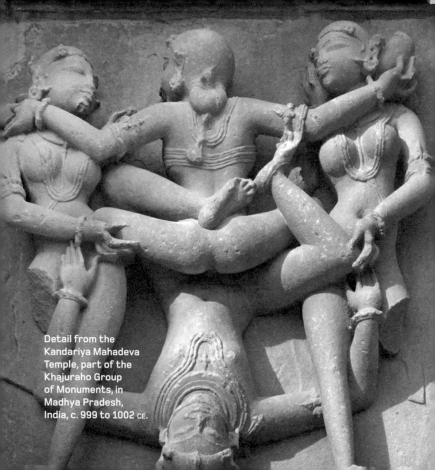

Detail from the Kandariya Mahadeva Temple, part of the Khajuraho Group of Monuments, in Madhya Pradesh, India, c. 999 to 1002 CE.

Romantic friendships and Boston marriages

From the late 19th century to the early 20th century in the United Kingdom and North America, Victorian dictates held that average white women were not very interested in sex outside their procreative duty to their husbands within marriage. Thus, white women were able to pursue various forms of intimacy with each other without it necessarily being seen as suspect. What scholars now refer to as 'romantic friendships' were rampant between women. These were incredibly close emotional relationships between women that could involve love letters, cuddling, kissing and sharing a bed. As long as the women involved went on to engage in heterosexual marriage, their relationships with other women often remained under the radar of social sanction.

'Boston marriages' involved two women living together in order to remain financially independent from men. Some of these arrangements would be classified as romantic friendships and even lesbian relationships today, while others were platonic, entered into for the purposes of pursuing a career.

Sarah Ponsonby and Lady Eleanor Butler, also known as the Ladies of Llangollen, lived together in what would later be termed a Boston marriage.

The first modern lesbian

Wealthy 19th-century English gentlewoman Anne Lister kept over two dozen diaries documenting her daily life, including her relationships with multiple women, which began in her youth at a girls' school. Her descriptions of sex with women were so explicit that they were thought to be a hoax before researchers confirmed their authenticity. Eventually Lister settled down with heiress Ann Walker, to whom she considered herself married. The couple lived at Shibden Hall, Lister's ancestral home, until Lister's death in 1840.

Lister's diaries were a treasure trove for scholars of gender and sexuality, as they provided the earliest written evidence of Western women having sex with each other. As a result, Lister has been called 'the first modern lesbian'. The passages in which she refers to her sex life were written in a complex code derived from algebra, Greek and the zodiac, further evidence of the stigma surrounding queer life in 19th-century Britain.

Portrait of Anne Lister by Joshua Horner, c. 1830. While townspeople called her 'Gentleman Jack' to ridicule her masculinity, Lister was affectionately called 'Fred' by her long-time sweetheart Mariana Belcombe.

Josephine Butler: crusade against sexual abuse

Born in 1828, Josephine Butler was an English social reformer and feminist who devoted her life to fighting against the sexual abuse of girls and women. In 1869 she began fighting to repeal the Contagious Diseases Act, which forced prostitutes to undergo routinized gynaecological exams to prove they were free from venereal disease. Butler decried these forced exams as 'steel rape'. In 1886, her efforts paid off, and the act was repealed. After founding the International Abolitionist Federation in 1875, she campaigned for similar reforms across Europe. The federation also held conferences with female and male attendees critical of how state regulation of prostitution negatively impacted sex workers.

Butler became an activist against child prostitution and sex trafficking. She also supported the movement for women's suffrage and the fight against coverture, a British legal doctrine in which women's legal rights were forfeited and subsumed under the rights of their husbands upon marriage.

US sculptor and feminist Abastenia St Leger
Eberle's commentary on child prostitution,
The White Slave, c. 1913.

Irish Magdalene laundries

From 1758 to 1996, Catholic-run, state-sanctioned Magdalene laundries exerted a powerful hold over the lives of at least 30,000 Irish girls and women. Based on the Catholic doctrine that women deemed sexually impure should repent for their 'sins', Magdalene laundries were billed as places to reform 'fallen women' (sex workers). Shunned from their communities, sex workers, and later unwed mothers, survivors of sexual violence and girls from reformatories, were sent to the laundries. Forced into hard labour for no pay, they were subjected to emotional, physical and sexual abuse by the nuns. The nuns also stole women's newborns, adopting them into Catholic households. The Magdalene women couldn't leave unless rescued by a male relative; thus, many were trapped there for life. Others escaped. In 1992, the discovery of a mass grave at the largest laundry sparked a public outcry, and the last laundry closed in 1996. The Irish government didn't issue a formal apology until 2013, when they set up a £50 million compensation fund for survivors. The Catholic church, however, refused to contribute.

Young girls and women working at an Irish Magdalene laundry in the early 20th century. Their duties included washing, starching and ironing church linens.

The Daughters of Bilitis

The 1950s were a decade of fear and oppression for lesbian and gay people in the United States. During the 'Lavender Scare', led by Senator Joseph McCarthy, lesbian and gay people were accused of being a threat to US civilization, and they were purged from federal government jobs. Homosexuality, as same-sex desire was then called, would be considered a mental illness by the American Psychiatric Association until 1974. Despite this oppressive environment, the US homophile movement formed to promote the toleration of gay and lesbian people. The male-dominated Mattachine Society was founded in 1950, and in 1955, lesbian women created the Daughters of Bilitis (DOB) in San Francisco. The DOB began as a secret social club with only eight members, including Phyllis Lyon and Del Martin, and established other small chapters across the United States and Australia. Early on, the DOB shifted towards a political focus on lesbian rights, becoming the country's first lesbian civil rights organization. Its members published *The Ladder*, the first long-running US lesbian magazine, from 1956 to 1972.

The Ladder

OCTOBER, 1957

Miss America protest

The year 1968 was one of protest and social unrest around the world. On 7th September, radical feminist group New York Radical Women organized a protest at that year's Miss America beauty pageant held in Atlantic City, New Jersey. A few hundred feminists, including key organizer Robin Morgan, protested at what they saw as the sexual objectification of women's bodies and the valuation of beauty over intelligence.

At the protest, women crowned a sheep Miss America, making the point that women were being appraised like livestock. They threw 'instruments of female torture' into a Freedom Trash Can, including bras, girdles, corsets, fake eyelashes, high-heeled shoes, curlers and copies of *Cosmopolitan* and *Playboy*. This portion of the event was erroneously reported in the media as 'bra burning' – likened to Vietnam War protesters' burning of their draft cards – and became mistakenly associated with the feminist movement for decades. However, as a result of the protest, feminism reached a national audience.

Women from the National Women's Liberation Party hold posters branding the Miss America event a 'cattle auction'.

The Stonewall Rebellion

In the 1960s, US police routinely raided gay bars and arrested patrons they found dancing together. Those arrested would have their names and faces published in the newspaper, after which they could be legally fired from their jobs. On 28th June 1969, New York City police raided the Stonewall Inn, a popular New York gay bar. After they bloodied a woman they put in handcuffs, she reportedly cried out to fellow LGBT customers, 'Why don't you guys do something?'

The crowd exploded. Homeless LGBT youths and poor and working-class drag queens and trans women of colour fought back against the police. Patrons started fires and threw pennies, bottles, bricks and rubbish bins at the police, who drew their guns. The fighting lasted several days, spurring the first gay pride protest the following year. The radical gay rights organization Gay Liberation Front was formed in 1970. The Stonewall Rebellion has been credited by many as inaugurating the modern-day US gay rights movement.

THIS IS A
RAIDED
PREMISES

POLICE DEP'T.
CITY OF NEW YORK
HOWARD R. LEARY. POLICE COMMISSIONER

Framed sign at the Stonewall Inn in New York from the 1969 police raid that caused the Stonewall Riots. In 2016 US President Barack Obama designated the Stonewall Inn a national monument.

Gloria Steinem

Gloria Steinem is known for her leadership in the feminist movement beginning in the late 1960s and early 1970s. A co-founder of *Ms.* magazine, Steinem first came to prominence through her feminist investigative journalism. As a freelance journalist during the 1960s, she examined the working conditions of Playboy bunnies in the Manhattan Playboy Club, applying to work as a bunny herself and going undercover for three weeks. She then wrote an article exposing the women's poor treatment, long hours, meagre pay and sexual degradation by the wealthy and powerful men who ogled them. In addition to helping found *Ms.* magazine, Steinem also co-founded the National Women's Political Caucus in 1971, which works to advance the number of women in politics. Two years later she founded the Ms. Foundation for Women, and in 2005 co-founded the Women's Media Center. She has long been involved in Democratic political causes and has been an advocate for ending violence against women. In 2013, US President Barack Obama awarded Steinem the Presidential Medal of Freedom.

Anne Koedt: 'The Myth of the Vaginal Orgasm'

Published in 1970, US radical feminist Anne Koedt's essay 'The Myth of the Vaginal Orgasm' rebutted the idea that women who couldn't orgasm through vaginal penetration alone were 'frigid'. To be frigid, as determined by the male-dominated medical field, meant that a woman was sexually 'abnormal' and required psychotherapy to become better sexually 'adjusted' to her husband. Koedt argued that the clitoris, not the vagina, is the seat of female sexual pleasure. Contrary to the teachings of Sigmund Freud, clitoral orgasms were not developmentally 'immature', wrote Koedt, but crucial for women's sexual satisfaction. According to Koedt, every female orgasm stemmed from the clitoris. Preventing the public from obtaining this knowledge, she argued, served to centre men's sexual pleasure at the expense of women's sexuality. Koedt's essay was transformational in advocating for a shift in how women thought about their own sexuality. In discarding the male-defined model that pathologized women's means of finding genuine sexual pleasure, Koedt created a new, clitoris-based model that remapped the terrain of sex.

Gustav Klimt, *Danae*, 1907

Germaine Greer:
The Female Eunuch

Controversial for some feminists, *The Female Eunuch*, published by Australian writer Germaine Greer, became a major text for 1970s feminism. In the book, Greer rejected consumerist culture and the nuclear family under capitalism, arguing that both instilled sexual repression in women. She suggested that, in having their vitality taken away by consumerism and capitalism, women were reduced to eunuchs. She declared that men actually hated women but that women didn't realize it, instead internalizing men's hatred by hating themselves. The only way out, Greer wrote, was anti-capitalist revolution. 'To abdicate one's own moral understanding … to leave everything to someone else, the father-ruler-king-computer, is the only irresponsibility,' wrote Greer. 'The opponents of female suffrage,' she added, 'lamented that woman's emancipation would mean the end of marriage, morality and the state; their extremism was more clear-sighted than the woolly benevolence of liberals and humanists … When we reap the harvest which the unwitting suffragettes sowed we shall see that the anti-feminists were after all right.'

Germaine Greer with a Dutch-language copy of her book, *The Female Eunuch*, in 1972.

The 'lavender menace'

In 1969, Betty Friedan, president of the National Organization for Women (NOW), allegedly declared lesbians a 'lavender menace' threatening the respectability of the US feminist movement. Heterosexual feminists during this time hoped to downplay the involvement of lesbians in feminism in order to avoid the charge that feminists were all 'man-hating' lesbians. That same year, at the First Congress to Unite Women in New York City, NOW dropped the New York chapter of the Daughters of Bilitis (see page 180) from its list of sponsors. In response, at the Second Congress to Unite Women in 1970, a group of radical lesbian feminists reclaimed Friedan's alleged slur by donning shirts that read 'LAVENDER MENACE' and interrupting the conference. They passed out copies of their manifesto 'The Woman-Identified Woman' and commandeered the microphone for an impromptu speakout on the problem of lesbian exclusion in feminism. The protest came to be recognized as a founding moment for lesbian feminism, and NOW adopted a resolution on lesbian issues at the following year's conference.

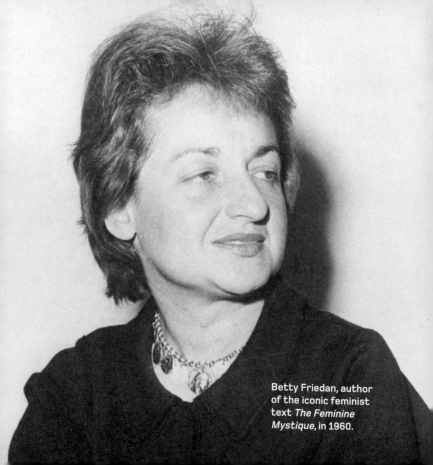

Betty Friedan, author of the iconic feminist text *The Feminine Mystique*, in 1960.

'The Woman-Identified Woman' manifesto

Published by the Radicalesbians in 1970, the manifesto 'The Woman-Identified Woman' opened with 'What is a lesbian? A lesbian is the rage of all women condensed to the point of explosion.' First distributed at the Second Congress to Unite Women (see page 192), the pamphlet was a founding document of radical lesbian feminism. Writing against the lesbiphobia of the feminist movement and in larger society, the Radicalesbians emphasized how lesbians were at the forefront of women's liberation. Their solution to men's oppression of women was for women to invest their energy in other women, including sexually. 'Until women see in each other,' wrote the Radicalesbians, 'the possibility of a primal commitment which includes sexual love, they will be denying themselves the love and value they readily accord to men, thus affirming their second-class status.' The Radicalesbians called women who put men's interests above their own 'male-identified'. In contrast, they argued, women must become 'woman-identified, as [o]nly women can give to each other a new sense of self'.

Leeds Revolutionary Feminist Group

Formed in 1977 and active through the 1980s in the United Kingdom, the Leeds Revolutionary Feminist Group (LRFG) was a radical lesbian feminist group that identified men's violence against women as a central component of women's oppression. The LRFG organized multiple 'Reclaim the Night' rallies around the country in 1977, which advocated for women's right to go out at night without having to fear sexual violence. The group joined other radical feminist groups in arguing that the 1960s 'sexual revolution' had been detrimental to women, as it asked women to have more sex with men without centring female sexual pleasure. In 1979, the LRFG published a pamphlet, 'Political Lesbianism: The Case Against Heterosexuality', which critiqued heterosexual vaginal penetration as a violation of women's bodies and a reminder of women's status as 'invaded centre'. Instead, the LRFG asked women to become political lesbians, which meant refusing to have sex with men, instead investing their energy in other women. While some political lesbians had sex with women, others were sexually abstinent or asexual.

Reclaim the Night rallies remain a legacy of LRFG activity. Here, comedian and political activist Kate Smurthwaite leads the chants at a rally in London in 2011.

Rape crisis centres

In the 1970s, feminists first coined the term 'rape culture' to describe how misogynist societies normalize men's sexual violence against women. The 1975 US documentary *Rape Culture* connected the issue of rape to sexism and violence against women, disputing the widely held belief that rape was rare. In 1978, the term 'rape culture' was first used in the US Congressional Record. It continues to be an important concept for feminists.

An early effort to fight rape culture occurred through the establishment of rape crisis centres. Feminists in San Francisco, California, established a part-time rape crisis hotline in 1973. In Australia, feminists opened the first rape crisis centre in 1974, and the UK's London Rape Crisis Centre was established in 1976. These centres provided an environment in which women could turn to other women for help. This was important because the male-dominated police and courts often disbelieved, retraumatized and slut-shamed survivors, in some cases covering up the sex crimes of friends and colleagues.

Feminist group Boston Feminists for Liberation protests at the State House in Boston, Massachusetts, against rape culture, 2012.

Erin Pizzey and the Chiswick women's refuge

Herself a survivor of family violence, English activist and writer Erin Pizzey opened the first women's refuge in the modern world in 1971. Located in Chiswick, London, Pizzey's refuge took seriously the concerns of 'battered' women and provided them with resources for economic survival and psychological healing. This was a revolutionary approach in an era when men's violence against women was generally considered to be a 'private affair'. In 1974, Pizzey wrote *Scream Quietly or the Neighbors Will Hear*, a book in which she highlighted the accounts of female survivors of domestic violence.

While most women who established women's refuges were radical feminists, Pizzey rejected feminism and remains a controversial figure for feminists. Accusing feminists of unfairly targeting men as the perpetrators of domestic violence, Pizzey argued (based in part on her own experiences of her mother) that women were just as capable of committing domestic violence as men.

1847 etching by George Cruikshank, illustrating the impact of alcoholism on men's domestic violence against women and children.

Erica Jong: *Fear of Flying*

In 1973, US writer Erica Jong published the novel *Fear of Flying*. It depicted the life of protagonist Isadora Zelda White Stollerman Wing, a 29-year-old Jewish journalist and poet. The novel explored Wing's affair with psychoanalyst Adrian Goodlove during a trip to Europe for a psychoanalysis conference. Using first-person perspective and a conversational tone, Jong revealed Wing's frank inner thoughts about her sexual desires, fantasies and domestic life. One of the novel's memorable incidents is Wing's fantasy of the 'zipless fuck' – casual sex between strangers.

When *Fear of Flying* was published, Jong's exploration of these themes was met with surprise, judgment and a devoted feminist following among women seeking sexual wholeness and freedom. It became an important novel for women. As Jong would later reflect, 'At the time I wrote *Fear of Flying*, there was not a book that said women are romantic, women are intellectual, women are sexual – and brought all those things together.'

The feminist 'sex wars'

During the 1970s and 1980s, as US feminists worked to articulate a vision of sexuality they could proudly call feminist, they often differed about what counted as patriarchal oppression. Two diametrically opposed camps engaged in what became known as the 'feminist sex wars'. Radical feminists such as Andrea Dworkin and Catharine MacKinnon argued that porn constituted violence against women and should be banned. They also argued that sex work exploited women and that BDSM (bondage, domination and sadomasochism) was anti-feminist. In contrast, 'pro-sex' feminists like Gayle Rubin and Pat Califia argued that women could explore their sexual freedom in multiple ways and that radical feminists didn't have a monopoly on feminist sexuality. The in-fighting came to the fore at the 1982 Barnard Conference on Sexuality. Angry that they hadn't been included on the steering committee, anti-porn feminists protested, passing out leaflets that decried the positions of many of the presenters. These disagreements continue to persist, illustrating how 'feminist sexuality' is a complex, heterogeneous subject.

Andrea Dworkin

Sex-positive feminism

Those who call themselves sex-positive feminists emphasize that just as 'no means no' and women should be free from rape culture, so, too, does 'yes means yes'. In other words, women's sexual autonomy and freedom are paramount issues for feminism. Sex-positive feminists challenge the anti-feminist stereotype that feminists view sex only in terms of patriarchy and danger.

US feminist sex educator, writer and porn director Tristan Taormino is one such feminist. Taormino, who is also a Feminist Porn Award winner, has built her career creating feminist porn. For Taormino, feminist porn emphasizes women's sexual pleasure, protects porn stars' rights as workers, promotes genuine versus tokenized diversity and gives performers autonomy in deciding what types of sexual scenes to engage in. Feminist pornographers like Taormino see feminist porn as a way of challenging the oppressive structures of the mainstream porn industry, including its exploitation of workers, sexual objectification of women, racism and ageism.

Jiz Lee, Lisa Vandever, Tristan Taormino (centre), Candida Royalle and Nenna Joiner at the 2013 CineKink NYC Film Festival.

The Shocking Pink Collective

Although published under the same name, *Shocking Pink* existed as two separate magazines. Both were produced by collectives of young London feminists – the first from 1980–1982 and the second from 1987–1992. The first ground-breaking collective gained a high profile and produced three issues positioned as an alternative to the hugely popular *Jackie* magazine, tackling serious issues rather than 'clothes and boys', and challenging traditional notions of femininity. The second collective, inspired and partly funded by the first, created a zine as part of the 1980s feminist resistance to the Conservative UK government. Both wrote about homophobia and bullying at school, racism, women's music and sex education. Many members were lesbian, and their work filled an important void in exploring lesbian youth issues. The second group paid special attention to railing against Clause 28, which prohibited UK authorities from 'promoting homosexuality'. As the riot grrl music scene reached the UK from the US in the early 1990s, *Shocking Pink* paved the way for other young feminist publications, such as *Bad Attitude*, *Subversive Sister* and *Girl Frenzy*.

YOU AIN'T SEEN NOTHING YET!

20p

SEXISM

SHOCKING
PINK

2nd Issue

Virginity, sexual shame and the 'purity myth'

It is common in patriarchal cultures to police female sexuality, with an emphasis on virginity as an indicator of sexual 'purity'. This is reflected in conservative Christian ideologies that associate premarital (heterosexual) sex with sin, sending girls the message that sexual exploration makes their bodies tainted and inferior. Feminists such as Jessica Valenti, author of *The Purity Myth*, have taken issue with how a young girl's self-worth becomes tied to her body and how those whose sexuality departs from the purity narrative become scorned. An event called the 'purity ball' has gained traction among US evangelical Christians. Relying on sexist ideas about 'purity' that disproportionately target girls versus boys, girls are sent to the balls with their fathers, where they sign a pledge to remain sexually abstinent until (heterosexual) marriage. In the meantime, they entrust their fathers with the 'safekeeping' of their virginity, and their fathers give them purity rings as symbols of this commitment to chastity. Many feminists, as well as women subjected to purity balls, have spoken out against these balls and the ideology behind them.

Fathers and daughters pray together at an annual Father-Daughter Purity Ball.

SlutWalk against slut-shaming

Speaking at a 2011 York University campus safety forum on rape, Toronto police constable Michael Sanguinetti said, 'I've been told I'm not supposed to say this; however, women should avoid dressing like sluts in order not to be victimized.' His words gained international media attention and Sanguinetti apologized, but for Canadian women and girls subjected to sexual violence and victim-blaming throughout their lives, this offered paltry comfort. That same year, Sonya Barnett, Heather Jarvis and others in Toronto founded SlutWalk, a march against victim-blaming and slut-shaming that has since spread to five continents. Declaring women's ownership of their bodies and right to sexual freedom, SlutWalk marchers chant, sing, dance and speak out about being survivors of sexual violence. Some dress in so-called 'slutty' clothes to emphasize how regardless of what a woman or girl is wearing, she is never asking for sexual violence. '[Sanguinetti] ... was talking about me ... you ... all of us,' wrote SlutWalk participant Clementine Morrigan in 2015. '[I]f we say it's okay to rape any of us then it's okay to rape all of us.'

The first SlutWalk protest in Toronto, 3rd April 2011.

The Gulabi Gang: 'Yes, we fight rapists'

The Gulabi Gang, also known as the Pink Sari Gang, is a group of women in rural northern India whose mission is to train women in self-defence against men's domestic and sexual violence. Founded by Sampat Pal in 2006, in the Banda District of Uttar Pradesh, the Gulabi Gang is comprised mostly of Dalit ('low'-caste) women who are routinely subjected to violence, poverty and child marriage.

Equipping women with long bamboo sticks called *lathis*, the Gulabi Gang empowers women in the face of the widespread corruption of the police and their failure to protect women from men's violence. The women use tactics such as dialogue, confronting and publicly shaming their abusers as a group, and martial arts to take justice into their own hands. Because of this, they're often referred to as a vigilante group. The group also provides financial resources for women in order to promote their economic self-sufficiency, which is crucial in freeing women from relying on abusive men for their day-to-day survival.

Members of the Gulabi Gang, also known as the Pink Sari Gang.

Coalition of African Lesbians

The Coalition of African Lesbians (CAL) was founded in Johannesburg, South Africa, in 2003. A network of 14 organizations in sub-Saharan Africa, it works in 10 different countries to support women's rights and to 'rais[e] consciousness amongst and strengthe[n] activism and leadership of lesbian women on sexuality and gender and its intersections with a wide range of lived realities'. CAL was founded to address the reality that women, especially lesbian women, are routinely denied a voice when it comes to leadership in social movements as well as policy decisions across Africa. Since 2010 they've expanded their reach from mostly regional to international advocacy. Members identify the group as an explicitly feminist organization, naming patriarchy as a central mechanism of oppression. The organization also takes an intersectional approach that recognizes how discrimination based on gender, sexual orientation and class are all connected. CAL's ultimate goal is to create a future Africa that is 'a place of power and justice', in their words, 'where social and economic justice are a reality for all people'.

Women participate in the 2006 Gay Pride
Johannesburg festival in South Africa.

Toxic masculinity and 'involuntary celibates'

According to Australian sociologist Raewyn Connell, hegemonic masculinity is a form of masculinity praised in patriarchal societies and based on men's subordination of women and other marginalized groups. Connell has written about how hegemonic masculinity relies on 'toxic' behaviours such as disparaging femininity, utilizing violence and repressing emotions other than anger. In his 2013 book *Angry White Men*, US sociologist Michael Kimmel illustrated how toxic masculinity is fundamental to the ideology of mass shooters who have expressed their hatred for women and/or feminism. This is true for Marc Lépine and Elliot Rodger: in 1989 Lépine killed 14 women and wounded 14 other people in Montreal, while in 2014, Rodger murdered six people and wounded 14 more in California. Rodger, and later mass shooters who praised him, identified as an 'incel', or 'involuntary celibate'. This term refers to a subculture of mostly white, heterosexual men who blame their lack of dating success on women, especially feminists. Incels exhibit physically and sexually violent attitudes towards women and are often virulently racist.

Monument in Victoria Park, London, Ontario, Canada, dedicated to the women murdered in the Montreal Massacre.

The 2017 US Women's March

On Inauguration Day 2017, following the election of Donald Trump to the US presidency, women and their allies protested in Washington, DC, and in over 650 other rallies throughout the United States. Anticipating the negative impact of Trump's presidency on the rest of the world, protests were also held in at least 81 other countries.

Referencing Trump's leaked audio tape in which he boasted about grabbing women 'by the pussy', many women donned pink 'pussy hats', holding signs such as 'PUSSY GRABS BACK' and 'Impeach the Sexual Predator'. According to *The Washington Post*, protests involved all major US cities and dozens of small towns alike, but were also recorded in even the most challenging of environments, including five people in a Los Angeles cancer ward, 50 women in a California nursing home and 2,000 people marching in Fairbanks, Alaska, despite the −40°C (−40°F) wind chill. In 2018, another Women's March was held to protest the first year of Trump's presidency.

The Women's March 2017, Washington. With 3.2 to 5.2 million participants, it was most likely the largest single-day protest in US history.

The #MeToo movement

In 2006, US black civil rights activist Tarana Burke became the unwitting founder of a global movement after using the phrase 'me too' to signal just how pervasive and real rape culture is for girls and women. Her phrase would resurface in 2017 on Twitter, as #MeToo became a transnational warrior cry for the tidal wave of sexual violence survivors who began sharing their stories publicly, often for the first time in their lives.

The #MeToo movement snowballed in the aftermath of the 2016 US presidential election, when Donald Trump emerged as the victor over Hillary Clinton, despite the emergence of audio tapes in which Trump bragged, 'I just start kissing [beautiful women] … I don't even wait. And when you're a star, they let you do it. You can do anything. Grab 'em by the pussy. You can do anything.' The movement gained steam as numerous high-profile men in US government, media and sports were accused and/or convicted of sex crimes. The movement continues as survivors storm the halls of power, demanding to be heard.

EU Parliament member Terry Reintke signals her support of the #MeToo movement at the European Parliament in Strasbourg, France during a 2017 hearing on preventing sexual harassment and abuse.

The exploitation of Sarah Baartman

The 19th-century exploitation of the Khoikhoi woman Sarah Baartman, argue modern feminists of colour, illustrates the early roots of the racist dehumanization, sexualization and 'othering' of black women's bodies. Born in the 1770s in what is now South Africa, Baartman was influenced to leave her country in 1810 and travel to Europe, probably under duress. She was exhibited in circuses and freak shows, becoming effectively enslaved. European obsession with Baartman's physical features, especially her pronounced buttocks, drove her exhibition, and large crowds influenced by the scientific racism of the time gathered to view her as an anthropological oddity. In France, she was even sold to an animal handler. After Baartman's death in Paris in 1815, she continued to be subjected to a prurient white gaze. Her remains – including skeleton, brain, genitals and a plaster cast of her body – were exhibited at French museums until complaints forced their removal in the 1970s. It wasn't until 2002 that South Africa succeeded in repatriating Baartman's remains for a dignified burial in her home country.

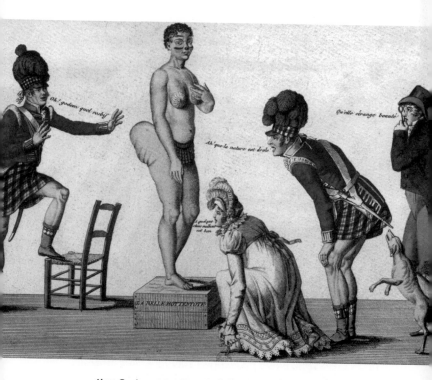

'*Les Curieux en extase ou les Cordons de souliers*',
a 19th-century satirical illustration of the European
obsession with Baartman's body.

The sexual economy of US slavery

The institution of slavery, as well as indigenous genocide and land theft, was foundational to the growth of white US wealth and the country's development as a superpower. For enslaved black women, their forced toil also included routinized sexual violence. White enslavers used rape as a weapon to terrorize black women and remind black men of their powerlessness to protect their families. Writing in 2002, legal scholar Adrienne Davis outlined how enslavers' mass rape of black women constituted a 'sexual economy' of white intergenerational wealth building.

After passage of the 1807 Act Prohibiting Importation of Slaves, Southern states focused on increasing their domestic supply by forcing black women and men to 'breed' as well as through enslavers raping the women themselves. Reproduction through rape also saved the enslavers money in having to purchase more people. New laws stipulated that an enslaved mother's child would also grow up enslaved, ensuring that enslavers' mixed-race offspring couldn't escape slavery.

Statue of Mary and Emily Edmonson — sisters freed from sexual enslavement in 1848, by sculptor Erik Blome in Alexandria, Virginia.

Harriet Tubman and the Underground Railroad

In *Scenes in the Life of Harriet Tubman*, written by Sarah Hopkins Bradford, Tubman is recorded as saying, 'I have heard their groans and sighs, and seen their tears, and I would give every drop of blood in my veins to free them.'

Born into slavery in Maryland, Tubman escaped to Philadelphia in her 20s, then returned to help her family members escape via the Underground Railroad, marking the beginning of her journey leading more than 300 people to freedom over 10 years. Travelling at night to avoid slave catchers, she used coded songs to alert her 'passengers' to potential danger as she approached them with food and supplies. During the Civil War, Tubman worked for the Union Army and led a raid at Combahee Ferry that liberated over 750 enslaved people. These acts of heroism earned her the nickname 'Moses'. Abolitionist Frederick Douglass wrote about Tubman in 1868, 'Excepting John Brown ... I know of no one who has willingly encountered more perils and hardships to serve our enslaved people than you have.'

Statue of Harriet Tubman in Harlem, New York. Faces, locks, chains, slave shackles and other items are visible in her skirt.

Sojourner Truth: 'Ain't I A Woman?'

Sojourner Truth was born into slavery in New York c. 1797. In 1826, forced to leave her other children behind, she escaped with her baby daughter Sophia. After suing the man she escaped from for illegally selling her son down to Alabama, in 1828 she secured her son's freedom. Truth's legal victory made her one of the first black women in the United States to win in court against a white man.

In addition to her abolitionism, Truth advocated for women's rights. She travelled to the Ohio Women's Rights Convention in 1851, where she gave her famous feminist speech later known as 'Ain't I A Woman?' Accounts of her speech vary, but what is known is that she challenged the notion of women as weak and delicate, reminding the white crowd that enslaved black women didn't have the privilege of being seen as dainty and incapable of work. Truth would go on to give many other speeches on abolitionism and women's rights. During the Civil War, she helped recruit black soldiers for the Union Army.

Sojourner Truth c. 1864

Sarah and Angelina Grimké

Born in Charleston, South Carolina, the Grimké sisters grew up in a prominent family that enslaved a large number of black people. After witnessing the horrors of slavery on their family's plantation, the sisters joined the abolitionist cause. Influenced by liberal Quaker beliefs on slavery and women's rights, they moved north to Philadelphia, where they became some of the first female public speakers in the United States. Decrying slavery, racism and gender inequality, Sarah and Angelina's speeches on the lecture circuit alienated them from Charleston high society and even from their Quaker community. Such experiences drew the sisters closer into the abolitionist fold. They wrote multiple tracts and books, such as Angelina's 'Appeal to the Christian Women of the South (1836)', which argued that slavery violated the US Declaration of Independence and the teachings of Christ. In 1839 the sisters edited the volume *American Slavery as It Is: Testimony of a Thousand Witnesses*. This volume had an important impact on the formation of the abolitionist movement and was quoted by luminaries including Frederick Douglass and Charles Dickens.

Wood engraving of Angelina Grimké

The feminist abolitionism of Lucretia Mott

Lucretia Mott was a 19th-century white Quaker abolitionist and women's rights activist born in Massachusetts. In line with her Quaker beliefs, Mott was ardently anti-slavery. She engaged in boycotts of products produced through slavery such as cotton and cane sugar. In 1821, Mott became a Quaker minister and travelled to give speeches against slavery, speaking to urban Northerners, Southern enslavers and President John Tyler alike. She then helped found the Philadelphia Female Anti-Slavery Society in 1833. This activism proved dangerous, as white mobs targeted her home as well as black neighbourhoods across Philadelphia. At the 1840 World Anti-Slavery Convention in London, men voted to ban Mott and the other female delegates from participating. Mott protested, and an Irish journalist called her the 'Lioness of the Convention'. She went on to organize the 1848 Seneca Falls women's rights Convention with her mentee, Elizabeth Cady Stanton, and became the first president of the American Equal Rights Association.

A marble statue of three suffragists
—Elizabeth Cady Stanton,
Susan B. Anthony and Lucretia
Mott (right)—by Adelaide Johnson
in the Capitol crypt, Washington, DC.

Gender and Jim Crow laws

In the post-Civil War United States, during the time period known as the Reconstruction era, white Southerners passed so-called 'Jim Crow' laws at local and state levels to reinforce racial inequality and segregation since they could no longer legally enslave black people. The laws lasted from the late 19th century to 1965, when the US black civil rights movement secured various legal victories against de jure racial discrimination. Historian Glenda E. Gilmore argued in her 1996 book *Gender and Jim Crow* that black women were uniquely impacted by the laws. After black men were disenfranchised at the turn of the century, wrote Gilmore, through white mob violence, poll taxes and literacy tests, black women became ambassadors to white America. Forming alliances with white women and engaging in feminist activism, including women's suffrage, helped black women advocate on behalf of their communities. Black women were trusted more by white America in their gendered role as nurturers, while black men, Gilmore argued, were construed as violent criminals.

Rosa Parks (right), pictured here with Coretta Scott King, was a key figure in challenging the legal structure of Jim Crow. Refusing to give up her seat on a Montgomery, Alabama, bus to a white passenger in 1955, she triggered the 381-day Montgomery bus boycott.

The Māori Women's Welfare League

The Māori Women's Welfare League was founded by Whina Cooper in Wellington, New Zealand, in 1951 — an organization dedicated to the empowerment of Māori women and families across New Zealand in the aftermath of settler colonialism. From World War II onward, Māori people increasingly began moving from rural areas to the cities, where they struggled to deal with racism, to adapt to a cash-based economy, and to secure housing and health care. The league, focusing on Māori women and children, sought to resolve these issues while preserving Māori culture and working with other New Zealand women's organizations. The league also had the distinction of being the first national Māori organization. In 1975, when she was 79, Cooper was asked to lead the Māori Land March on behalf of Māori land rights. Cooper agreed, heading a group of 5,000 protesters, who marched across the entirety of North Island to parliament in Wellington. On arrival, Cooper presented New Zealand Prime Minister Bill Rowling with a petition signed by 60,000 people in support of Māori land rights.

The 1975 Māori Land March, which was led by Māori Women's Welfare League founder Dame Whina Cooper.

Olive Morris: The Brixton Black Women's Group

Olive Morris was born in Jamaica in 1952, immigrating with her family to Britain when she was nine. While she tragically died of cancer at age 27, she nonetheless fiercely fought for black civil rights and women's rights as a socialist community organizer and activist. For example, as a 17-year-old she reportedly tried to intervene in anti-black police brutality against a Nigerian diplomat, suffering a severe beating and arrest from police. Morris was active in Britain's Black Panther movement during the late 1960s and early 1970s, a time of rampant oppression against African, Afro-Caribbean and Asian communities in Britain. These groups faced discrimination in housing and employment, attacks by the fascist political party the National Front and tension with police, all of which culminated in the 1981 Brixton uprising in South London. Within this environment, Morris co-founded multiple groups, notably the Brixton Black Women's Group (1973), which later became the Black Women's Centre. It focused on black women's issues, including motherhood and securing resources for economic survival.

Brixton riots, 1981

The Combahee River Collective Statement

Active from 1974 to 1980, the Combahee River Collective was a Boston-based black lesbian feminist organization. Co-founder Barbara Smith named the group based on the 1863 raid at the Combahee River in South Carolina by Harriet Tubman (see page 228). In 1977, the group wrote the Combahee River Collective Statement, which set out a vision of feminist liberation based on black lesbian feminist socialism. The document is important for its critiques of both the racism found in white-dominated US feminism and the sexism in US black liberation movements. The statement also identified capitalism and imperialism as central to the oppression of women. Writing that '[a]ll systems of oppression are interlocking', the statement's authors illustrated the importance of simultaneously analyzing gender, race, class and sexuality in an era before intersectional feminism had been coined as a term. They famously argued, 'If Black women were free, it would mean that everyone else would have to be free since our freedom would necessitate the destruction of all the systems of oppression.'

Named after a military campaign that freed over 750 black people from slavery, the Combahee River Collective sought to free black men and women from their struggle against racism and sexism.

This Bridge Called My Back

The 1980s was a decade for the flourishing of feminist scholarship and activism by US women of colour. Responding to what had been a largely white-dominated, middle- to upper-class feminist movement, feminists of colour took it upon themselves to call out the racism in the feminist 'sisterhood' and to build a feminist movement responsive to their own needs and experiences. An early book to do this work was the 1981 anthology *This Bridge Called My Back: Writings by Radical Women of Color*. Edited by Chicana feminists Gloria Anzaldúa and Cherríe Moraga, and currently in its fourth edition, the book is lauded for its accessible language and use of storytelling. It calls upon white feminists to incorporate race into their analysis of oppression, and it gives voice to the experiences of prominent feminists of colour related to race, class, sexuality and gender. Gathering the narratives of Asian-American, black, Chicana/Latina and Native American women into one cohesive anthology promoted solidarity between feminists of colour and the book has become one of the most-referenced texts in feminist theory.

Cherríe Moraga, co-editor with Gloria Anzaldúa of *This Bridge Called My Back*.

Audre Lorde's *Sister Outsider*

Written in 1984, Audre Lorde's *Sister Outsider: Essays and Speeches* was a defining text for black feminism and women of colour feminism more broadly. Lorde wrote in the context of working within a feminist movement that proclaimed 'sisterhood' while continuing to make black women and lesbians feel like outsiders. She drew attention to this paradox in the title of her work, digging into difference as a source of strength and power. In *Sister Outsider*, Lorde explored many themes, including racism in white-dominated feminist circles and black women's internalized racism. She threaded her discussion of black female empowerment with an attention to lesbian sexuality and included cutting-edge work on motherhood from the perspective of being a lesbian woman in an interracial relationship. Lorde also discussed ageism and US imperialism. *Sister Outsider* produced some of the most powerful quotes in feminist theory, including 'Women are powerful and dangerous', 'The master's tools will never dismantle the master's house', and 'Your silence will not protect you'.

Audre Lorde,
self–described
'Black lesbian
feminist warrior
poet mother'.

Grace Lee Boggs' civil rights activism

In her 1998 autobiography *Living For Change*, civil rights activist Grace Lee Boggs wrote, 'Had I not been born female and Chinese American, I would not have realized from early on that fundamental changes were necessary in our society.'

Boggs was born in Providence, Rhode Island, in 1915 to Chinese immigrants. After earning her PhD in 1940, she was inspired by black labour activist A. Philip Randolph, and decided she wanted to dedicate her life to activism. Boggs became involved in many major movements, including labour, civil rights, black power, women's rights and environmental justice. In the 1960s she joined the Black Power movement along with her husband James Boggs. During their 40-year marriage, the couple worked together as activist equals. Grace was a firm supporter of grassroots activism and pursued many projects in her adopted cities of Chicago and Detroit, including founding a youth organization called Detroit Summer. 'Revolution,' she said, 'is evolution toward something much grander in terms of what it means to be a human being.'

Artistic rendition of a young Grace Lee Boggs

The South African anti-apartheid movement

Under apartheid, from 1948 to 1994, the white supremacist National Party of South Africa came to power and instituted laws that codified racial segregation across society. In 1952, the African National Congress began a campaign of resistance that culminated in Nelson Mandela's 1994 presidential victory.

An important figure in the anti-apartheid movement was Patricia McFadden, an African feminist sociologist, activist and educator born in Swaziland in 1952. McFadden agitated against apartheid for over 20 years. She is also a former editor of the *Southern African Feminist Review*. Writing about the role of women in the movement against apartheid, McFadden argued that African women 'have been in the forefront of anti-colonial struggles ever since we were colonized'. African women, she wrote, fought apartheid equally alongside men, from feeding their communities in the midst of violence and economic crisis to participating in guerilla warfare against the Nationalist Party.

Apartheid-era sign in both English and Afrikaans.

Winona LaDuke: indigenous feminist activism

Ojibwe activist and author Winona LaDuke was born into a family descended from Anishinaabe spiritual leaders on her paternal side and Jewish labour activists on her maternal side. She is known for her environmental activism on behalf of indigenous communities through two non-profit organizations she founded, Honor the Earth and the White Earth Land Recovery Project. The former promotes awareness of and fundraises for issues of environmental justice in Native American communities. The latter purchases land back from non-native people on the White Earth Ojibwe Reservation in Minnesota. In 1985, LaDuke helped found the US-based non-profit Indigenous Women's Network (IWN) with Janet McCloud. IWN was founded in part as a reaction to the sexism pervading the indigenous rights movement of the 1980s. The group produces *Indigenous Women*, the first and only magazine written by and for indigenous women. LaDuke also ran as the vice presidential candidate alongside consumer rights activist Ralph Nader for the US Green Party in 1996 and 2000.

Winona LaDuke (left) and Grace Roberts, an enrolled member of the Mille Lacs Band of Ojibwe, perform a jingle dance during the Enbridge Energy Pipeline 3 protest at Kellogg Mall Park, St Paul, Minnesota.

Missing and murdered indigenous women

In Canada, the issue of missing and murdered indigenous women (MMIW) has been described as a hidden crisis. For decades, indigenous community members have protested the lack of resources allocated to its investigation. In British Columbia, a rural portion of highway known for hitchhiking and the abduction of indigenous women since 1969 was nicknamed the 'Highway of Tears'. Bordering 23 First Nations communities, this highway has been host to numerous murders of low-income indigenous girls and women, most of which remain unsolved. Assembly of First Nations regional chief Cameron Alexis has called MMIW 'a national shame and a national tragedy'.

After decades of activist work, the Royal Canadian Mounted Police released findings in 2014 stating that between 1980 and 2012, 1,181 indigenous women had gone missing or been found murdered across Canada. The next year, Prime Minister Justin Trudeau announced the creation of a National Inquiry into Missing and Murdered Indigenous Women and Girls.

Canadian Prime Minister Justin Trudeau, giving a speech on missing and murdered indigenous women in 2016. At the time, according to statistics from the Canadian Institute for Identities and Migration, one-quarter of Canadians held negative views about indigenous people.

Black Lives Matter and #SayHerName

In 2013, black feminist activists Patrisse Cullors, Alicia Garza and Opal Tometi founded the Black Lives Matter movement as a clarion call against routinized anti-black police brutality and murder in the United States. The women began using the hashtag #BlackLivesMatter after vigilante George Zimmerman was acquitted in the Florida murder of black teenager Trayvon Martin. The hashtag then reached a nationwide audience after police officer Darren Wilson shot Michael Brown dead in Ferguson, Missouri, and after New York City police officers choked Eric Garner to death. Black Lives Matter has since become an international movement. After the mysterious 2015 death of Sandra Bland – a black woman found hanging in a jail cell three days after being arrested during a traffic stop in Texas – the hashtag #SayHerName sprang up on social media. In contrast to Black Lives Matter activism that focuses mostly on the male victims of police brutality, #SayHerName draws attention to the situation of black women, including the high rate of murder against black trans women.

Black Lives Matter protesters in 2015.

Sacred fertility

Representations of the sacred feminine can be traced to the ancient past. In the case of the Venus of Willendorf – an 11.1cm (4.4in) statue estimated to have been made c. 30,000 BCE, and part of a category of Palaeolithic statues found across Europe dubbed 'Venus figurines' – no one is sure exactly of its original significance. Among the most prominent hypotheses is that the Venus of Willendorf was used in fertility rituals, that it represented a Mother Goddess, or that it, and other figurines like it, may have been self-portraits of ordinary women.

Regardless of the murkiness as to its original use, the Venus of Willendorf has been cherished by modern feminists for decades, both as a symbol of the importance of women in ancient art and religion, and also due to its representation of voluptuous womanhood. Modern scholars of fat studies have pointed to the Venus of Willendorf's curves as an example of how fatness has been honoured and even revered, in this context as a potential reminder of (most) women's ability to generate life.

Side and front views of the Palaeolithic figurine known
as the Venus of Willendorf, found in Lower Austria in 1908.

Lilith: wife, demon, feminist icon

A complex figure, Lilith has been subjected to the fears and desires of many groups of people. In the medieval Jewish text *Alphabet of Ben Sira* (often interpreted as satirical), Lilith is alleged to be Adam's first wife, created by God from the same material as Adam. After Adam rejected Lilith's request to be treated as his equal, Lilith refused to be subservient and to lie under him during sex, instead flying away. God then created Eve from Adam's rib as an appropriate 'helpmate'. In Isaiah 34:14, the Hebrew *lilith* or *lilit* is translated as 'night hag' or 'screech owl', and indeed Lilith has, over the centuries, been conceptualized as a sexual demon who preys on men at night and steals and eats babies. Feminists have connected this demonization to Lilith's refusal to submit to patriarchal control. In 1976, the magazine *Lilith* was created, and its tagline, 'Independent, Jewish & Frankly Feminist', endures to this day. The 1990s women's folk music festival Lilith Fair, founded by Canadian singer Sarah McLachlan, was also named for Lilith. Some neopagans and witches venerate her, celebrating her independence and sexual power.

Representation of Lilith by artist Ernst Barlach, c. 1922.

Yeshe Tsogyal

Known as the Mother of Tibetan Buddhism, Yeshe Tsogyal was, according to legend, an enlightened woman who lived during the eighth and ninth centuries. She is thought by Tibetan Buddhists to be a reincarnation of Buddha's mother, Maya. Born a princess, Tsogyal wanted to pursue spiritual study instead of marry, and even ran away, but was caught and forced to wed the emperor of Tibet and live in his harem. After the emperor invited the master Guru Rinpoche to come to Tibet from India to spread Buddhism, he gave Tsogyal to Rinpoche as a token of appreciation. Rinpoche freed Tsogyal, and she became his consort and main disciple. Tsogyal studied under Rinpoche and became her own spiritual master and teacher, with both male and female disciples. After spending nine years in an isolated meditation retreat and accomplishing various tantric spiritual achievements, Tsogyal reached enlightenment. She is considered a female Buddha, and is also revered as a manifestation of Saraswati, the Hindu goddess of wisdom, and sometimes as Tara, the Mahayana Buddhist bodhisattva.

Tibetan Buddhist nuns take part in a prayer ceremony to Yeshe Tsogyal at Gebchak Nunnery, Tibet, Nepal.

The Vestal Virgins

In ancient Rome, the Vestal Virgins (also called simply Vestals) were priestesses of the goddess Vesta, who ruled the home and hearth. Their priestesshood made them privy to secret rituals denied to male priests, and it spanned over a thousand years, lasting from the eighth century BCE to the fourth century CE.

Inside the Temple of Vesta, the Vestals kept Vesta's sacred hearth fire continuously lit. Entering into service to Vesta as children, they served for 30 years and took a vow of chastity. Exempt from marriage and childbirth, they instead officiated over religious events, made food for rituals, gathered water from a sacred spring, and guarded public documents and the wills of powerful Romans. Because Vesta's flame came to represent the Roman state, the Vestals were seen as key to maintaining the prosperity and strength of Rome. They had various rights unusual for Roman women to possess, such as the right to own property and to bequeath it to other women, and could free enslaved people and prisoners by touching them.

The House of the Vestal Virgins in Rome, Italy.

Hildegard of Bingen

Born c. 1098 CE in what is now Germany, Hildegard of Bingen was an abbess (a type of honoured leader of nuns) known for her mystical visions. She reportedly experienced visions since childhood, collecting them into three books. Bishops came to her for guidance and she interacted with the Pope – forms of respect that were essentially unheard of for women in the Catholic church during Hildegard's lifetime.

In addition to her religious work, Hildegard of Bingen was an accomplished poet and musical composer. Her music is still available for listening and has influenced New Age music. She was a veritable Renaissance woman before the age of the Renaissance, instructing helpers to dictate her writings on topics as diverse as the lives of the saints, natural history and herbal medicine in addition to her own prophecies. Hildegard of Bingen was canonized as a saint in 2012, based on the miracles she was said to have performed in her life as well as her veneration by the public.

1998 sculpture of Hildegard of Bingen by Karlheinz Oswald, located at Eibingen Abbey in Germany.

The 'heresy' of Jeanne d'Arc (Joan of Arc)

Jeanne d'Arc was a 15th-century French peasant who claimed to hear angelic voices from a young age. These voices told her she was destined to save France from English occupation, as the Hundred Years' War was raging across the land. Despite living in an era in which the Catholic church brutally oppressed anyone who challenged its authority, and in which it was virtually unheard of for women to become military leaders, Jeanne convinced Charles VII of France that she was on a divine mission to save the French people. She went on to successfully raise an army to drive the English from their occupation of multiple French cities. The price Jeanne paid for resisting her society's norms was steep. She was tried, convicted and burned alive for heresy in 1431; she was just 19 years old. Her persecution for heresy, like the persecution of many women for related crimes, was motivated by political interests and male resentment at a woman transgressing her allotted social role. In 1920, through a bittersweet twist of irony, the Catholic church declared Jeanne d'Arc a saint.

Gender and witch hunts

For centuries in Europe and North America, the figure of the witch has been associated with unbridled female power and sexuality. Whether depicted as the bride of Satan, a demon's consort or as a circle of naked women dancing together around a bonfire, Western ideas about witches have been intimately connected to social anxieties about gender, sexuality, religion, class conflict and power. Scholars estimate that between the 16th and 18th centuries, some 50,000 people were murdered as witches, 75 to 85% of them women. Many accused of witchcraft acted as healers or midwives in their local communities, using plant knowledge to create herbal brews and salves. Others were accused out of spite, jealousy, attempts at seizing their property (for the few that owned property) or even for being seen as too sharp-tongued. While almost none of those persecuted as witches actually viewed themselves as witches, modern-day feminists continue to look to the witch hunts and the figure of the witch as evidence of the fear and hatred of strong women.

Sor Juana Inés de la Cruz

Born in what is now Mexico c. 1650, Sor (Sister) Juana Inés de la Cruz has been called the first published feminist of the New World. She entered a nunnery in 1667 in order to devote her life to scholarship and avoid marriage, in the process becoming a great author of the Hispanic Baroque period and a celebrated poet, philosopher, playwright and composer. Fluent in Latin and Nahuatl, she accomplished all this while being self-taught. In her convent room, Cruz cultivated one of the biggest libraries in the New World at that time.

Cruz's attention to women's rights in her writing was bold. In her poem *'Hombres necios'* ('Foolish Men'), she rebuked men for their efforts at casting women as illogical, turning the tables to illustrate how men were illogical. Her plays centred on strong women, and based on her romantic poetry to other women, scholars have argued that she was probably lesbian. After a priest tried to silence her and deny education to women, Cruz wrote a treatise, *La Respuesta* (The Answer), combatting his arguments.

V. R. D. L. M. R. M. Juana Ynes
de la Cruz, Fenix de la America,
Glorioso desempeño de su Sexo,
Honrra de la Nacion de este nuevo
Mundo, y argumento de las admi
raciones, y elogios de el Antiguo.
Nació el dia 12 de Nov. de el año de
1651. à las onze de la Noche. Reci
vió el Sagrado Habito de el Maximo
D. S. S. Geronimo en su Conv.to de
esta Ciudad de Mexico, de edad de
17 a.s y murió Domingo 17 de Abril
de el 1695. de edad de 44 a.s cinco
mezes cinco dias, y cinco horas

Requiescat in pace. Amen.

Portrait of
Sor Juana Inés
de la Cruz,
attributed to
Juan de Miranda.

Anne Hutchinson and religious freedom

In the dour Massachusetts Bay Colony, female preacher, midwife and herbalist Anne Hutchinson was an anomaly. Raised by a nonconformist Puritan minister who taught her to read, Hutchinson held Bible sessions for local women in her home. She spread the teachings of Puritan minister John Cotton among the women, attracting many more followers to his cause. In so doing, she challenged the male-dominated religious authorities, especially given their disdain for Cotton's unorthodox ideas.

Hutchinson developed the idea that anyone could reach heaven through having a personal relationship with God. She also argued that sin didn't impact whether someone went to heaven or hell. These ideas contradicted Puritan teachings. The Puritan leadership declared her a heretic in 1637 and banished her and her family. The Hutchinsons sought refuge in Rhode Island, then New York, where Anne and most of her family were killed by indigenous warriors. Her legacy remains one of female religious leadership and steadfast conviction on behalf of religious liberty.

Anne Hutchinson on trial, as portrayed by artist Edwin Austin Abbey in 1901.

Nana Asma'u, Nigerian Muslim leader

Born in 1793 in what is now northern Nigeria, Nana Asma'u is a revered figure in contemporary Nigeria, where she is honoured as an ancestor of modern African feminism. She was the daughter of Usman dan Fodio, founder of the Sokoto Caliphate and devotee of the mystical Islamic tradition of Sufism. Dan Fodio believed in universal education for both men and women. He trained his daughter in Qur'anic studies, and she, like many other female members of her family, played a prominent role in the literature and politics of the Sokoto Caliphate.

Asma'u became a scholar of classical texts and later advised her brother when he succeeded their father in the caliphate. Over the course of 40 years, she wrote more than 60 texts, covering histories, poetry and women's rights under Islamic law. She was particularly devoted to women's education. Asma'u trained female teachers, who drew on her scholarship and taught female students in their homes. She continues to have northern Nigerian buildings, organizations and schools named after her to this day.

Nana Asma'u's legacy continues to exert an important influence on contemporary Nigerian women and African Muslim feminists.

Marie Laveau, Voodoo Queen

Marie Laveau, dubbed the Voodoo Queen of New Orleans, was a well-respected voodoo priestess in 19th-century Louisiana. Born in the French Quarter of New Orleans c. 1801 to Marguerite Henry, a free woman of colour, and Charles Trudeau dit Laveau, a white politician, Laveau became known for her ability to heal the sick and intervene in the fortunes of her clients. She provided them with advice, candles, powders and magical gris-gris bags to conjure change in their own lives. Gathering with initiates at her home on St Ann Street, at Congo Square, and on the shore of Lake Pontchartrain, Laveau presided over rituals involving singing, dancing, drumming and spirit possession. In this way, she became a shrewd businesswoman, amassing a network of wealthy and powerful clients who consulted her on a range of issues. As a woman of colour working to survive and thrive during the dehumanizing and dangerous era of enslavement in the American South, Laveau created a legacy of power, magic and mystery that lives on in present-day New Orleans, where she remains a beloved and popular figure.

Marie Laveau (seated), with her daughter, in the last year of her life. She was supposed to be over 100 years old.

Paula Gunn Allen's The Sacred Hoop

Written in 1986, *The Sacred Hoop: Recovering the Feminine in American Indian Traditions* was a groundbreaking text that unearthed the rich matriarchal spiritual traditions of North American tribal communities prior to colonization. Native American poet Paula Gunn Allen suggested that, in relearning the key leadership roles their female ancestors played spiritually, socially and politically, contemporary indigenous women would be able to excavate the spiritual power denied to them under European conquest. Allen argued that European colonizers' destruction of indigenous cultures had much to do with patriarchal fear of women having decision-making power across all segments of society. She analyzed how patriarchal views of gender were a European importation rather than stemming from indigenous communities. While some scholars have critiqued Allen as homogenizing indigenous cultures and offering a romanticized vision of indigenous matriarchy, her work was key in establishing indigenous feminist scholarship in the 1980s.

Paula Gunn Allen's work encourages indigenous women to rediscover the pro-women cultural roots that prevailed before the age of patriarchal European invasion.

Feminism and theosophy

The Theosophical Society was founded in New York City in 1875 as an occult movement claiming to be premised on 'the universal brotherhood of humanity without distinction of race, creed, sex, cast, or colour'. Similarly in Canada, prominent early feminists Emily Stowe, Augusta Stowe-Gullen and Margaret Denison helped found the Canadian Theosophical Society in 1891. Theosophy incorporated Western occultism with Eastern religions, especially Hinduism and Buddhism, and was a predecessor to Western New Age movements. It emerged at a time in North American and British history when movements such as spiritualism were popular. According to historian Joy Dixon in her 2001 book *Divine Feminine: Theosophy and Feminism in England*, many English feminists had strong ties to theosophy and saw their feminist activism as the manifestation of a spiritual crusade. The Theosophical Society participated in various progressive causes, including sending contingents to feminist marches, such as the pro-suffrage Women's Coronation Procession held in London in 1911.

Helena Blavatsky and Henry Steel Olcott, the two main founders of the Theosophical Society, pictured in 1888.

When God was a woman

In 1976, US art historian and sculptor Merlin Stone published *The Paradise Papers: The Suppression of Women's Rites*, republished as *When God Was A Woman*. Stone explored the widespread existence of goddess-worshipping religions in antiquity prior to the rise of monotheistic, patriarchal Judeo-Christian theology. She argued that the Hebrews and Christians violently overpowered peaceful, matriarchal religious traditions in order to replace the sacred feminine with the sacred masculine, causing massive imbalance and destruction leading up to present times. Stone's text has been critiqued for its totalizing claims about matriarchal religions and the extent to which they were uniformly peaceful. However, her work inspired the development of feminist theology and the revival of goddess worship in the 1970s and 1980s. Feminist theologians inspired by Stone's research reinterpreted their religious traditions, questioning male-centred imagery and ideas about God, while turning their attention to the women in their sacred texts and the women-centred traditions that preceded their faiths.

The Siddur Nashim and feminist Judaism

The Siddur Nashim was the first Jewish prayer book to use female pronouns and imagery to refer to God. Published by Maggie Wenig and Naomi Janowitz in 1976, the Siddur Nashim was part of the renaissance of feminist theology and Jewish feminism in the 1970s. Jewish feminists during this time challenged their exclusion from all-male prayer groups and their inability to begin divorce proceedings in Jewish religious courts, among other grievances. While some liberal Jewish traditions now draw on female words and imagery for speaking about God, others use gender-neutral pronouns, and ensure that Jewish prayer book references to the patriarchs Abraham, Isaac and Jacob equally reference matriarchs Leah, Rachel, Rebecca and Sarah.

US Rabbi Rebecca Trachtenberg Alpert has said about the Siddur Nashim, 'The experience of praying with Siddur Nashim ... transformed my relationship with God. For the first time, I understood what it meant to be made in God's image.'

The Jewish prophetess Miriam leading the women around her 'with timbrels (tambourines) and with dances', included in the Tomic Psalter, a holy Bulgarian illuminated manuscript, c. 1360–1363 CE.

Feminism and Dianic Wicca

In the 1970s, goddess worship saw a resurgence among feminists who were re-evaluating their ideas about religion and their place in the cosmos. Many women were drawn to the idea of a religion that centred women and the sacred feminine. As a result, Dianic Wicca was born – an offshoot of Wicca, the English pagan religion established by Gerald Gardner and others in the first half of the 20th century.

Wicca incorporates pre-Christian Celtic religious practices with elements of other esoteric and occult movements. While a basic tenet of Wicca is the dualistic worship of the God and Goddess, Dianic Wiccans, named after the Roman goddess Diana, focus exclusively on the Goddess. Hungarian-American high priestess Zsuzsanna 'Z.' Budapest was a main figure in the creation of Dianic Wicca, forming the Susan B. Anthony Coven, the first feminist, women-only coven. Dianic Wiccan rituals are conducted through a distinctly feminist lens and include healing from patriarchal violence, binding rapists and celebrating the female body.

A pagan altar paying homage to the Mother Goddess.

The French hijab ban

In 2004, the French government targeted French Muslim schoolgirls in its first ban on the hijab. The government justified its ban by pointing to the policy of *laïcité*, or secularism, which stipulates that there must be a strict separation between church and state in French society. The government also argued that banning Muslim schoolgirls' hijabs was necessary to protect girls from being controlled by their male relatives. Some French feminists have supported bans on the hijab, as well as later bans on the niqab, arguing that the bans protect women's equality in French civil society. Other feminists, however, decry the bans as Islamophobic. They argue that it's condescending to presume Muslim women can't make decisions for themselves. Still others have pointed out that, in practice, *laïcité* upholds double standards around religion. For example, visible markers of Islam are banned, yet obvious symbols of Christianity, such as nuns' habits, don't face nearly the same level of public scrutiny and backlash. There has reportedly been an increase in hate crimes against Muslims in France since the introduction of the bans.

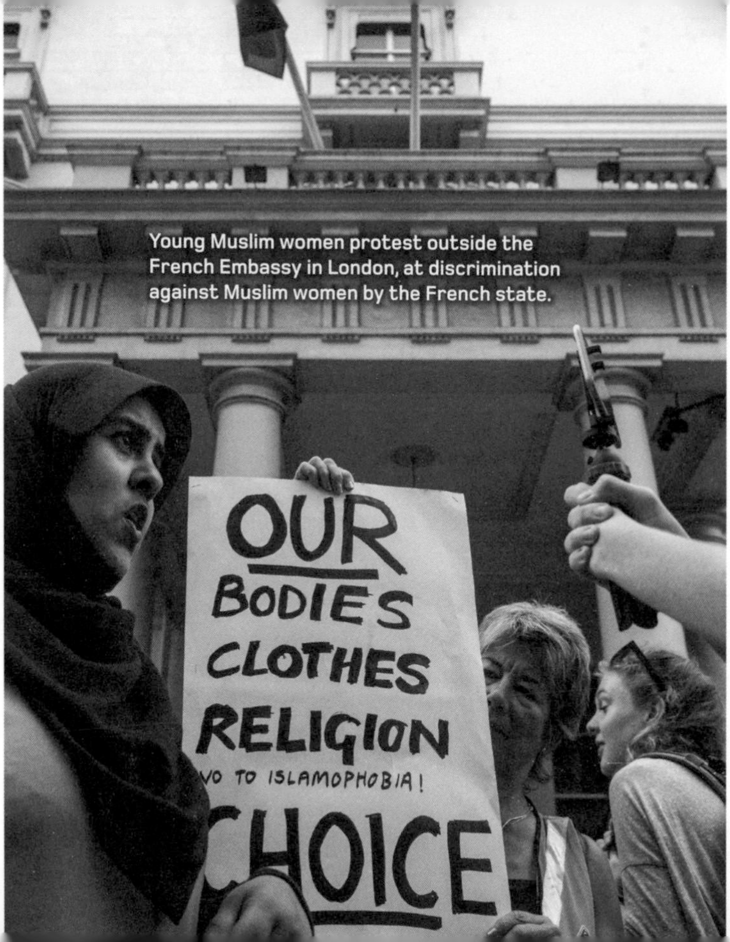

Young Muslim women protest outside the French Embassy in London, at discrimination against Muslim women by the French state.

OUR
BODIES
CLOTHES
RELIGION
NO TO ISLAMOPHOBIA!
CHOICE

Mormon feminism

Mormonism, founded in 19th-century New York, is known both for its historical embracing of polygamy and its strict gendered rules for men and women. It's not typically associated with feminism. However, in recent years growing numbers of vocal Mormon feminists have sought to change the church from within, making it more equitable and friendly to women and LGBTQ+ people. They also seek a greater acknowledgement of the Heavenly Mother, a divine female figure in Mormonism, who serves as humans' spiritual mother as well as God's wife.

Mormon feminist Kate Kelly experienced firsthand the struggles of trying to bring gender equality to the Mormon church. In 2013 Kelly founded Ordain Women, an organization advocating that Mormon women be eligible for the church's priesthood. Ordain Women generated much interest from like-minded women, and Kelly led a protest at the Mormon headquarters in Salt Lake City, Utah, in April 2014. That June the church excommunicated Kelly, indicating the leadership's ongoing resistance to feminist change.

Kate Kelly

Feminist witchcraft in the 21st century

The early 21st century has seen a resurgence in witchcraft, from the witches of 1990s popular culture to the incorporation of 'witchy' spirituality into fourth-wave feminism. Many millennial-aged and 'Generation Z' women and non-binary people have turned to pagan spirituality in the face of the global financial crisis, austerity measures, white supremacist and anti-immigrant movements, and the devastating impacts of climate change. Members of W.I.T.C.H., an anonymous activist witches' group based on the 1960s US feminist group of the same name, have protested against the policies of US President Donald Trump.

Many Latina women have embraced the pre-Christian spiritual heritages of their ancestors, as well as the practices of religions blending folk magic with Christianity, such as Santería. These women have reclaimed *brujería*, the Spanish word for witchcraft, embracing the sacred feminine in a culturally resonant way, an important task within witch communities often dominated by white women.

Members of W.I.T.C.H. Boston hold signs counterprotesting a white supremacist rally on 19th August 2017.

Greek Amazons as feminist warriors

In Greek mythology, the Amazons were female warriors said to dwell on the coast of the Black Sea. The Greek poet Homer described them as 'the equal of men'. Daughters of the war god Ares, the Amazons created an all-female society whose only intimate contact with men was for annual reproductive purposes. They raised female offspring and either killed or sent male infants to be raised by the all-male Gargarean tribe with whom they reproduced. Young Greek women in the ancient city of Ephesus were said to pay homage to the Amazons by performing an annual circular dance with shields and weapons that had been established by Amazonian queen Hippolyta.

In the 1970s, radical lesbian feminists drew on the Amazons for inspiration. These feminists used the labrys, a double-headed axe associated with the Amazons in ancient Roman Crete, as a symbol for matriarchy and female self-sufficiency and power. The lesbian feminist art journal *Amazon Quarterly* (1973–74) is one of many examples of the feminist legacy of the Amazons.

Amazons fighting Greeks, from a frieze at
the Mausoleum of Halikarnassos c. 350 BCE.

Boudicca, Queen of the Iceni

Born c. 30 CE, Boudicca was a Celtic queen, and likely Druid priestess, of the Iceni tribe in eastern Britain. In 43 CE, the invading Romans conquered southern Britain and razed the Druids' sacred groves. When Boudicca's husband, Prasutagas, died without a male heir in 60 CE, the Romans took his kingdom and publicly flogged Boudicca and raped her two daughters. This was done not only to terrorize Boudicca's family but to inspire submission in the whole tribe. According to Roman historian Tacitus, Boudicca declared, 'Nothing is safe from Roman pride and arrogance. They will deface the sacred and will deflower our virgins. Win the battle or perish, that is what I, a woman, will do.' Calling upon the war goddess Andraste for victory, Boudicca launched a massive attack on the three Roman centres of power in Britain, including London. After killing 70,000 Romans and pro-Roman Britons, Boudicca's army was defeated in their last battle before ultimate victory. She and her daughters poisoned themselves to evade capture. Boudicca's memory survives in Britain, where she's regarded as a folk hero and, for many, a feminist icon.

Statue to Boudicca in London, England

Andrea Smith's *Conquest*

Native American studies scholar Andrea Smith's book *Conquest: Sexual Violence and American Indian Genocide* (2005) became a classic text in indigenous feminism. Smith argued that white colonizers used rape as a central tool of genocide. Colonization, Smith wrote, has also had profound impacts on indigenous family structures and the ability of indigenous women to parent their children in a secure, culturally appropriate environment. In particular, Smith explored the legacy of Indian boarding schools, which operated in North America during the 19th and 20th centuries. Christian missionaries were paid to strip indigenous children of their 'savage' cultures and languages at the schools. Over 150,000 children were sent to Canada's schools, and at least 6,000 died from starvation, disease and forced medical experiments. Abuse was rampant, and dozens of mass graves have since been uncovered. Cultural genocide, alcoholism and suicide, as well as creating an entire generation of people unsure of how to parent having grown up without parents, remain the schools' legacies.

A group of Apache Indians after attending Carlisle Indian school for four months.

Hawaiian women under colonization

The 19th-century colonization of Hawaii was an immeasurable blow to the respected status and autonomy of indigenous Hawaiian women. Prior to colonization, sovereign Hawaii was a centre for women's leadership. There were female chiefs in Hawaii since 1375, and Hawaiian religion paid homage to goddesses as much as it venerated gods. The hula dance, meanwhile, was a source of women's profound spiritual power.

After US missionaries brought Christianity to the islands in the 1800s, however, Hawaiian women were forced to adopt 'Christian' names with patrilineal surnames. The missionaries used their influence to launch an attack on women's sexuality, leading to sexual behaviour outside monogamous heterosexual marriage becoming criminalized. The sacred hula became hypersexualized and legally regulated before ultimately being exploited for US-controlled tourism after the forced removal of Queen Lili'uokalani in 1893 and the complete US takeover of the territory.

Hawaiian nationalist and professor Haunani-Kay Trask has argued that the white-dominated tourist industry's commodification of Hawaiian women's sexuality through hula has led to the cultural prostitution of Hawaii.

Gender and Orientalism

Orientalism refers to the Western, homogenized, racist fantasy of the 'East' that views Eastern cultures as exotic, mysterious and culturally inferior. It serves to justify colonialism and imperialism, as Western powers can claim they're 'civilizing' the cultures they invade. Looking at the intersections between Orientalism and gender shows us how Asian women have been locked into racist and sexist tropes in the Western imagination. One stereotype, that East Asian women are either obedient, naive 'lotus blossoms' or seductive, sly 'dragon ladies', emerged from the history of Western military aggression. During the Korean and Vietnam Wars, the US military set up brothels, exploiting the local women desperate for money after having their economies and infrastructure destroyed. Through this limited contact, the stereotype of the hypersexual Asian woman was transmitted through Western popular media. In response, Asian and Middle Eastern feminists have fought back. As spoken word artist Suheir Hammad retorts, 'The beat of my lashes against each other ain't some dark desert beat — it's just a blink. Get over it.'

The term 'Orientalism'
was coined by
Palestinian theorist
Edward Said in 1978.

Arab Women's Association of Palestine

Palestine remains one of the only Middle Eastern peoples without a formally recognized sovereign nation, and issues of nationalism have long dominated women's movements there. After the British took over during World War I and declared support for establishing a Jewish state in Palestine, an armed, male-led resistance movement followed. The British violently suppressed the revolt, paving the way for Israel's creation in 1948. In the 1920s, women were active in the nationalist struggle, believing that gender equity would follow from securing a free Palestinian state. Over 200 women met in Jerusalem in 1929 to convene the Palestine Arab Women's Congress, which later became the Arab Women's Association (AWA). From then until 1948, AWA women marched in protests, established local women's associations, confronted government officials, delivered speeches, raised money for weapons and sometimes engaged in combat. While the AWA didn't call themselves 'feminist', they challenged gender norms to create a Palestinian liberation movement organized and led by women.

A woman walks carrying a jug with a child during the forced exodus of over 700,000 Palestinians from their homes during the creation of the state of Israel in 1948. The ensuing war was known in Arabic as *Al Nakba*, 'The Catastrophe'.

The sexual enslavement of 'comfort' women

Between 1932 and 1945, the Japanese military abducted some 200,000 women from across Southeast Asia, forcing them into sexual slavery in brothels called 'comfort stations'. They did this as part of their attempt to take over China and other portions of Asia, with the goal of terrorizing the women and symbolically 'castrating' the men in the countries they invaded. The infamous 1937 Rape of Nanking, in which Japanese soldiers raped between 20,000 to 80,000 Chinese women, is but one example of imperial Japan's mass dehumanization and sexual abuse of women. It's estimated that 90% of the comfort women didn't survive the war. But for those who did, scores were left infertile by the sexual violence, and the emotional trauma has been immense. Survivors have had to fight socially imposed stigma to speak up about their experiences, with many committing suicide. Groups supporting the 'comfort' women have since sprung up in multiple countries. Advocates of the women continue to question the Japanese government's commitment to full accountability.

The bronze statue of a comfort woman in front of the Japanese Embassy in Seoul, South Korea. Many comfort women were initially lured into thinking they were being offered educational or job opportunities.

Sophie Scholl: The White Rose anti-Nazi movement

Born in 1921 to a liberal politician critical of Hitler, Sophie Scholl began questioning the Nazis, especially after enrolling at the University of Munich with her brother Hans and meeting fellow artists, philosophers and writers.

After finding a pamphlet from the White Rose – a nonviolent, anti-Nazi group recently formed at her university by a small cluster of students and a professor — Scholl joined the group, which included Hans, as its only core female member in 1942. She helped write, copy and distribute pamphlets urging Germans to passively resist the Nazis.

However, in February 1943, the Gestapo arrested the group's core members and sentenced many of them to death, including Scholl. Among her last words were, '[W]hat does my death matter, if through us, thousands of people are awakened and stirred to action?' That same year, Allied air forces would drop millions of copies of the White Rose's last pamphlet across Germany.

A waxwork of Sophie Scholl, Madame Tussaud's, Berlin, Germany.

Women in the Algerian Revolution

Between 1830 and 1847, the French invaded and colonized Algeria, committing a 'scorched earth' policy of massacres and mass rapes. The Algerian people resisted, waging guerrilla warfare against the French for a number of years. From 1954 to 1962, the Algerians waged a successful war for independence known as the Algerian Revolution.

During the war, thousands of Muslim Algerian women fought for their country's independence, mostly in the National Liberation Front (FLN), a socialist political party that constituted the major nationalist movement during the war. Both urban and rural women joined or supported the FLN. A small percentage participated in attacking French military and civilian targets. These attacks gained global notoriety, especially the violence committed by women like Djamila Bouhired during the 1957 Battle of Algiers. Bouhired planted bombs targeting French civilians, but was spared from the guillotine due to an international outcry. She has been called 'the Arab Joan of Arc'.

In the 1966 film *The Battle of Algiers*, which was banned in France upon its release, Algerian women go undercover to help wage war against the French occupation of their country.

Women and the Sandinistas

In 1912, the US military occupied Nicaragua in order to build a canal to improve trade routes. In response, the Nicaraguans formed a resistance movement led by Augusto César Sandino. The Americans left in 1933, and from 1936 to 1979 the Somoza family ruled Nicaragua in a dictatorship until being forced out in the Nicaraguan Revolution. The socialist Sandinista National Liberation Front (FSLN), who took their name from Sandino, powered the revolution.

Women played prominent roles at all levels of the FSLN, including in combat and command positions, 'something unprecedented in Latin American history', according to author Norma Stoltz Chinchilla. By 1987, women constituted an estimated 67% of active members of the popular militia and 80% of the guards. Under the Sandinistas, women's educational opportunities increased, working women were equipped with training programmes, child care programmes were instituted, and women's participation and leadership in politics increased.

EL DEBER DE UN HOMBRE ES ESTAR ALLI, DONDE ES MAS UTIL

JOSE MARTI

An FSLN propaganda poster

Ministerio de Educacion
CRUZADA NACIONAL DE ALFABETIZACION

Feminism at the US–Mexico border

The US–Mexico border has been a place of violence and conquest since at least 1848, when the United States invaded Mexico and took about one-third of its land. Those whose ancestors had lived in the area for thousands of years were subjected to racism and xenophobia, often while being separated from their families by the new border. This oppression continues. Chicana feminist writer Gloria Anzaldúa explored issues of home, exile, belonging and identity at the border in her 1987 book *Borderlands / La Frontera: The New Mestiza*. She drew on the idea of the borderlands as geographic borders, but also as borders between cultures. She discussed *mestiza* identity – women with mixed indigenous and Spanish heritage – within the historical context of conquest and rape. While *mestizas* often felt as if they could never be fully embraced by either culture, Anzaldúa wrote, developing what she termed *mestiza* consciousness would allow all their disparate parts to coexist. They could then decolonize their minds from the 'either/or' logic of colonization, war and white supremacy.

Under Anzaldúa's theory of *mestiza* consciousness, Chicana women are encouraged to find empowerment through embracing their status as existing in between cultures.

'Collateral damage': language and war

Given that language helps construct social reality, its use in wartime is something that interests feminist scholars. In her 1987 article 'Sex and Death in the Rational World of Defense Intellectuals', Carol Cohn immersed herself in the world of defense intellectuals – those (in Cohn's experience, all men) who created the policy around managing nuclear weapons. Defense intellectuals, Cohn found, created terms that distanced them from the actual carnage on the ground. 'Collateral damage', for example, was an effective substitute for talking about the murder of innocent people, and 'surgically clean strikes' brought a cold sterility that left out the messy reality of mangled limbs and screaming mothers. Cohn also discovered that the defense intellectuals employed misogynist metaphors invoking sexual violence to describe war, such as missiles 'penetrating' the ground, shooting missiles into the 'nicest holes' and referring to an exploded bomb as 'losing her virginity'. The longer Cohn immersed herself, she found, the more desensitized she became – precisely the goal of creating such language in the first place.

Carol Cohn's work asks us to resist making the torture and murder of human beings during war into an abstract and easily-digestible concept.

Women in Black:
anti-war activism

Founded by Israeli women in Jerusalem in 1988, shortly after the start of the First Intifada (the Palestinian rebellion against the Israeli occupation of the West Bank and Gaza), Women in Black is a global women's anti-war movement. Its name comes from the black clothing worn by the women every Friday during their vigil to mourn the victims of Israeli human rights abuses in the occupied Palestinian territories. The group spread to other cities across Israel, and eventually to other countries. Members do not share a common set of beliefs beyond standing together against the Israeli occupation. While groups in other countries were initially founded in solidarity with women in Israel and Palestine, over time, they've organized around issues impacting their own communities as well, such as genocide in 1990s Yugoslavia, right-wing Hindu violence against women in India, and domestic violence in Australia. Women in Black holds an annual international conference to connect members around the world. In 2001, the United Nations awarded them the Millennium Peace Prize for Women.

Members of Women in Black protest in 2012 with a banner reading 'End the Occupation' in Hebrew, Arabic and English in Paris Square, Jerusalem.

Greenham Common Women's Peace Camp

In 1981, upon learning that the British government intended to house 96 nuclear missiles at the Greenham Common military base in Berkshire, England, female anti-nuclear activists marched from Cardiff, Wales, to Greenham Common in protest. They then decided to set up an encampment. A few months later, they organized 'Embrace the Base', in which 30,000 women formed a human chain around the base's 15.5km (9-mile) perimeter. Disrupting various nuclear missions, dozens of women were arrested. But they kept coming back – in even higher numbers, with hundreds of arrests – and inspiring women's encampments elsewhere in Europe. Emphasizing their identities as mothers, the women continued their encampment for 19 years – one of the longest feminist protests in history. Though often demonized in the media, the women influenced the removal of the site's last missiles in 1991, remaining at the base until they could ensure the land would be returned to the public. This happened in 1997. The last women finally left the camp in 2000, after winning the right to construct a memorial at the base.

Embracing the base at Greenham Common, 1982.

Malala Yousafzai: defying the Taliban

On 9th October 2012, Malala Yousafzai was returning home from school when a Taliban gunman shot and critically wounded her. She was 15 years old. Raised by humanitarian parents, Yousafzai had been an outspoken advocate of girls' right to an education since she was a child. In response, the Taliban issued a death threat against her. After her attempted assassination, however, Yousafzai made a remarkable recovery. Rather than backing down, she launched an international career as an activist for women's and girls' education.

In 2013, just one year after being shot, and on her 16th birthday, Yousafzai gave a speech to the United Nations. She published her bestselling book *I Am Malala* the same year. In 2014, Yousafzai won the Nobel Peace Prize at age 17, becoming the youngest person ever awarded the honour. Her organization The Malala Fund raises money for girls in several countries to attend school. In 2015 the fund opened a school for Syrian refugee girls in Lebanon.

'Corrective' rape in South Africa

South Africa has one of the highest rates of rape in the world, and out of every 25 men tried for rape, 24 walk free. In 2015, the South African charity Luleki Sizwe reported that, each week, rapists attack more than 10 women, committing either rape or gang-rape. According to the South African Institute of Race Relations, rapists will attack at least 40% of South African women over the course of the women's lives.

'Corrective' rape is a hate crime in which rapists target lesbians, pledging to 'turn' them straight. Often the women are murdered. Rapists also target women perceived as gender non-conforming for corrective rape, illustrating how homophobia and rigid gender norms go hand in hand. Corrective rape, argue feminists, is an example of men's violent entitlement to women's bodies. The crisis also shows how, despite South Africa's progressive post-apartheid legal protections for gay and lesbian people, forward-thinking policies do not necessarily translate into equity and safety on the ground.

Festival-goers at Soweto Pride participate in a die-in to protest violence against lesbians. Supporters hold a 'Dying For Justice' banner and wear shirts that read 'Solidarity with women who speak out'.

#BringBackOurGirls

On 14th April 2014, members of the Nigeria-based terrorist group Boko Haram – whose name means 'Western education is sinful' – kidnapped 276 schoolgirls from their school in the Nigerian town of Chibok. Women and girls who escaped later reported that the terrorists raped them and forced them into marriages even when they were underage.

Within days of the kidnapping, Nigerian accountant and prominent banker Obiageli 'Oby' Ezekwesili gave a speech, arguing that Nigerians must do something tangible to 'bring back our girls'. Lawyer Ibrahim Abdullahi mentioned Ezekwesili on Twitter the same month, agreeing with him and writing '#BringBackOurGirls'. That was the first use of the #BringBackOurGirls hashtag, which soon went viral.

In 2014, 57 girls escaped, and between 2016 and 2018, dozens of girls were found or rescued. Over 100 girls and women remain missing, and over a dozen are feared dead.

US First Lady Michelle Obama shows her support for the #BringBackOurGirls campaign in 2014.

Kurdish women of the Peshmerga

The Peshmerga ('those who face death') are the military forces of Southern Kurdistan. Kurdish warriors have been fighting for their independence for thousands of years, but have at times also split into competing factions. These factions united in 2003 to help defeat the regime of Saddam Hussein. More recently, they've been instrumental in the fight against terrorist group ISIS, also known as 'Daesh' in the Middle East. Margret George Malik, active in the 1960s, is believed by many to have been the first female Peshmerga. In the fight against ISIS, Peshmerga women have taken to the frontlines, with an estimated 1,700 women serving in combat roles in 2017. ISIS, virulently misogynistic and known to force women into sexual slavery, are allegedly infuriated by having to fight women. Female Peshmerga fighter Avin Vaysi told journalists in 2016, 'I saw on television that Daesh is torturing women and it made my blood boil . . . I decided to go and fight them.' Male Peshmerga commander Hajir Bahmani added, 'We are 100% equals. We are proud of the women fighters.'

Peshmerga women in 2008

Hypatia of Alexandria

Philosopher, mathematician and astronomer Hypatia was born c. 350-370 CE in Alexandria, Egypt, then part of the Eastern Roman Empire. A respected intellectual who became a widely renowned teacher of philosophy and science, Hypatia eventually headed the Neoplatonic School of Alexandria.

Before Julius Caesar conquered Alexandria in 48 BCE, the city was a flourishing centre of learning. During Hypatia's lifetime, tensions grew between the pagan, Christian and Jewish populations. Hypatia, being pagan, nonetheless was esteemed by many Christians. In 412 CE, the Christian extremist Cyril became Alexandria's ruler. He engaged in a feud with the governor, Orestes, who was also an associate of Hypatia's. In 415, a mob of Christian monks accosted Hypatia's carriage, dragged her into a church, ripped off her clothes and brutally murdered her. Many people at the time conjectured whether Cyril ordered her murder, a question scholars continue to debate. Today, Hypatia's legacy lives on in the naming of the feminist philosophy journal *Hypatia*.

Midwifery

Women assisting other women in childbirth extends back to antiquity and historically included knowledge of herbs and folk remedies. During medieval times, midwives were attacked as possible witches due to their knowledge of herbs, especially abortifacients. Because midwives held power in bringing forth life, when women lost babies during childbirth, sometimes midwives would be blamed as intentionally causing harm through witchcraft.

In the 18th century, the rise in the authority of male-dominated science fields created a schism between the supposedly capable, scientific male doctors and the 'alternative medicine' of the female-dominated world of midwifery. Feminists have seen this as men dismissing and attempting to usurp women's traditional sources of power. In contemporary Western medicine, midwives have legitimized their presence by establishing guidelines for the training and certification of 'nurse-midwives'. Modern midwifery departs from the medical model in viewing birth as natural and normal rather than emphasizing danger.

Ancient Roman relief carving of a midwife
helping a woman who is giving birth.

19th-century sexology and gender

In the late 19th and early 20th centuries, German and English medical professionals developed sexology to scientifically study human sexuality. This was part of a larger push to apply scientific principles to human populations, which often resulted in justifying human prejudice through science. Sexologists, researching and writing during the sexually repressive Victorian era, paid particular attention to those deemed sexually abnormal by society. They hoped to study sexual 'deviance' to understand what caused it, how to fix it and, sometimes, to cultivate more empathy in society for those afflicted. As part of their analysis, sexologists fixated on women's bodies. Using existing sexist norms for how women 'should' behave, sexologists created new medical labels for women who didn't conform to the rules. Women deemed too sexual became nymphomaniacs, women who rebelled against their husbands became hysterics and women attracted to other women were called sexual inverts. While some people found these labels helpful, feminists came to understand them as ways to control and medicalize women's bodies.

When British poet and novelist Radclyffe Hall published her iconic 1928 lesbian novel *The Well of Loneliness*, sexologist Havelock Ellis agreed to write the foreword as a medical professional in support of tolerating 'sexual inverts', the name then given to lesbians and gay men.

Women's treatment in insane asylums

In her 1972 book *Women and Madness*, US feminist author and therapist Phyllis Chesler suggested that the male-dominated fields of psychology and psychiatry have historically used sexist parameters to determine which women counted as 'healthy' versus 'insane'. In doing so, she argued, they conveniently disposed of women who refused to comply with the behaviour expected of them. According to data gathered between 1869 and 1872 at one Wisconsin asylum, reasons given for admitting women included 'domestic troubles', 'overexertion', 'suppressed menses', 'loss of property', 'nymphomania' and 'abortion'. In 1887, journalist Nellie Bly went undercover at the Women's Lunatic Asylum at Blackwell's Island in New York City, feigning insanity to get admitted. Her resulting book, *Ten Days in a Mad-House*, documented widespread abuse, spoiled food, dirty drinking water, exposure to the elements and the imprisonment of women clearly not insane. As a result of Bly's testimony, a grand jury investigated, and the state increased the budget for asylums, pledging to more carefully screen those admitted.

Women being held at the
Ohio Insane Asylum in 1946.

Florence Nightingale

Florence Nightingale was born to a wealthy English family who expected her to perform the duties of a young Victorian society woman. However, she wanted to be a nurse, and she lamented women's lack of control over their lives as 'an evil in the world'. In 1851, Nightingale was finally able to travel to Germany for nursing school. Two years later, the Crimean War broke out, and Nightingale, freshly trained, tended to the wounded and dying soldiers with a bedside lamp that became iconic in later representations of her. She was also a trained statistician, was fluent in five languages and pioneered sanitation and public health efforts in the United Kingdom as well as in British-occupied India, Pakistan and Bangladesh. In 1860 Nightingale founded the Nightingale School for Nurse Training, the first school to provide women with scientific, rigorous nursing training. Her school led to Nightingale being called the founder of modern nursing, and through her work, nursing became established as a key way for women to pursue a career in an era in which their options for economic independence were extremely limited.

A lithograph after the painting by Henrietta Rae, c. 1881 to 1891. It shows Florence Nightingale with her lamp at a patient's bedside during the Crimean War.

Anna Kingsford and animal rights

English social reformer Anna Kingsford is best known for her work on behalf of animal rights, anti-vivisection and vegetarianism. Born in 1846, Kingsford moved to Paris to pursue her medical degree, one of very few women. She reportedly completed her degree without engaging in any animal experimentation. Kingsford experienced blatant sexism in medical school, including a professor who refused to call her name while taking roll, telling her she was 'neither man nor woman'. Experimentation on animals without anaesthesia was in its heyday, including by prominent men such as Louis Pasteur. Kingsford wrote about her time at medical school, 'I was sitting in … the school, with my head in my hands, trying vainly to shut out of my ears the piteous shrieks and cries which floated incessantly towards me up the private staircase … I prayed, "Oh God, take me out of this Hell…"' Using her rigorous medical training to rethink humans' place in the hierarchy of life, Kingsford provided foundational arguments for a cause that ecofeminists, animal liberationists and vegans continue to agitate for today.

Medical experimentation on women of colour

Doctors have long experimented on women of colour through coercion and by failing to obtain informed consent.

James Marion Sims, called the 'father of modern gynaecology', perfected his 19th-century surgical techniques experimenting on enslaved black women without anaesthesia and guided by the racist belief that black people couldn't feel pain. He subjected an 18-year-old woman named Lucy to an hour-long bladder surgery, during which she screamed and cried out in pain, as other doctors watched. Once anaesthesia became available, Sims experimented on white women, illustrating how white women have been afforded humanity at the expense of women of colour.

In Puerto Rico, in 1955, US eugenicist Clarence Gamble – heir to Procter & Gamble – tested a version of the birth control pill on low-income Puerto Ricans. Although the women knew the drug they were given prevented pregnancy, they didn't know they were part of a clinical trial or that the drug was experimental.

In April 2018, this statue erected in honour of James Marion Simms was removed from New York's Central Park following a review into 'hate symbols'.

SURGEON &
PHILANTHROPIST
FOUNDER OF THE WO
AN'S HOSPITAL STATE OF
W YORK HIS BRILLIANT
HIEVEMENT CARRIED
E FAME OF AMERICAN
RGERY THROUGH-
OUT THE ENTIRE
WORLD.

BORN 181

FIRE OGNITION
OF HIS SERVICES IN
THE CAUSE OF SCIENCE
& MANKIND AWARDED
HIGHEST HONORS BY HIS
COUNTRYMEN & DECOR
ATIONS FROM THE GOV
ERNMENTS OF BELGIUM
FRANCE ITALY SPAIN
& PORTUGAL

DIED 1883

J. MARION SIMMS

M.D. L.L.D.

Margaret Sanger and birth control

Born in 1879, US social reformer, nurse, sex educator and writer Margaret Sanger grew up in a home with ten siblings, whom she helped raise from a young age. Her mother underwent 18 pregnancies in 22 years, then died aged 49. As a nurse, Sanger met many working-class women who didn't have proper knowledge of how to control their pregnancies. One woman, Sadie Sachs, died in front of Sanger after attempting a self-induced abortion. Spurred into action, Sanger popularized the term 'birth control' and opened the first US birth control clinic in 1916, for which she was arrested and put on trial for obscenity. Sanger also founded the American Birth Control League, the organization that became Planned Parenthood. Convinced that the fight against poverty was connected to the fight for birth control, Sanger endorsed negative eugenics, in which, as she put it in 1921, 'the mentally and physically defective' – people with mental illness, those with physical disabilities, and people in extreme poverty – shouldn't reproduce. Because of these views, Sanger remains an important, yet flawed and polarizing, figure in feminism today.

Flora Murray: The Women's Hospital for Children

Scottish suffragette Flora Murray earned her medical degree in 1905 and a diploma in public health the following year. After joining the Women's Social and Political Union (WSPU) suffragette organization in 1908, she served as the WSPU's doctor, giving speeches, participating in rallies and marches, and providing first aid during protests. Murray also gave medical assistance to suffragettes who had been force-fed in prison after undergoing hunger strikes, and she, along with some colleagues, advocated against force-feeding imprisoned people.

In 1912, with her partner Louisa Garrett Anderson, a fellow doctor and WSPU member, Murray founded the Women's Hospital for Children. The hospital's motto was 'Deeds Not Words' and was devoted to providing health care for poor and working-class children. It also enabled female doctors in London to acquire clinical training in pediatrics. Murray died in 1923 and lies buried next to Anderson, whose grave reads, 'We have been gloriously happy'.

Black women's contributions to space

Women working as 'human computers' – those who calculated complex equations in the era before electronic computers – have been employed since the late 19th century. Black women were first hired as human computers in the United States during World War II. While performing the same work as white employees at the National Advisory Committee for Aeronautics (NACA, the precursor to NASA), black women were paid less, forced to work in segregated facilities and were typically passed over for promotions. Nonetheless, in 1948, Dorothy Vaughan became NACA's first black supervisor.

After the creation of NASA in 1958, Mary Jackson became its first black female engineer the same year. Katherine Johnson, who had worked at NACA and then NASA since 1953, performed trajectory calculations that enabled astronauts to land on the Moon in 1969. Johnson would go on to work at NASA until 1986, and in 2015 was honoured with the Presidential Medal of Freedom.

Mary Jackson, one of the three prominent black female mathematicians and scientists at NASA profiled in the book and film *Hidden Figures*, at work in 1980.

Rosalind Franklin and the structure of DNA

Born in 1920 in London, Rosalind Franklin showed scientific promise from a young age. She eventually studied chemistry at the University of Cambridge. However, because Cambridge refused to award women BAs and MAs until 1947, she didn't receive her degree until six years after she graduated. After earning her PhD, Franklin worked at King's College London, where, in 1953, she concluded that DNA is formed as a double helix. Other scientists in Franklin's lab showed her work to James Watson and Francis Crick, who had drawn similar conclusions at a different lab. Watson, viewing Franklin's work as confirming work of his own, hurriedly published an academic paper with Crick in the journal *Science*. Watson and Crick's paper became the first published work on the structure of DNA, overshadowing Franklin's work. Franklin died five years later of ovarian cancer, and for many years her work on DNA went unrecognized. In 1962, when Watson, Crick and Franklin's colleague Maurice Wilkins won the Nobel Prize in Chemistry, Franklin wasn't acknowledged. But today, her legacy as a trailblazing woman in science lives on.

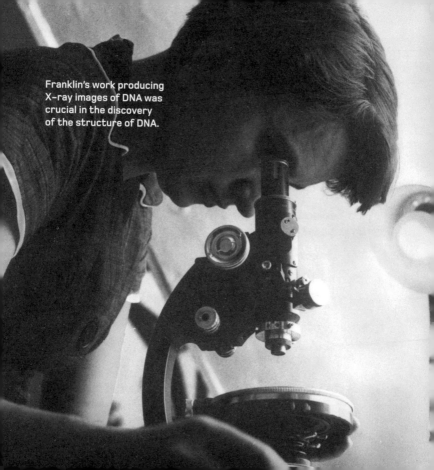

Franklin's work producing X-ray images of DNA was crucial in the discovery of the structure of DNA.

Anne Fausto-Sterling's *Sexing the Body*

In her 2000 book *Sexing the Body*, feminist geneticist Anne Fausto-Sterling challenged societal assumptions about sex and gender using biological research. Focusing on intersex children (those who are born with genitalia that doesn't neatly fit into 'male' or 'female'), she argued that, due to chromosomal variations, five sexes exist. However, because society is uncomfortable with sexual ambiguity, doctors typically surgically 'correct' intersex infants' genitals at birth.

In deciding who to 'slot' as male or female, argued Fausto-Sterling, doctors may rely on cultural beliefs masked as objective science. Doctors, seeing infants with protruding genitals that could be a small penis or large clitoris, assume that initiating penetrative heterosexual sex is most important for men, and perform surgery marking the child as male. For women, they assume that giving birth is more important than sexual performance, and so perform surgery to mark an infant with a uterus as female.

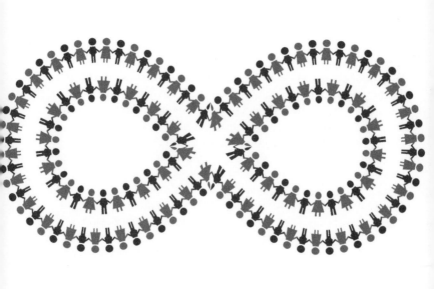

Sappho, poet of Lesbos

Born on the Greek island of Lesbos c. 630 BCE, Sappho was a prolific and widely-praised poet who wrote poems designed to be sung with the accompaniment of a lyre. Tragically, despite writing eight or nine volumes of poetry, most of her work has been lost, in part due to the fact that she wrote in an Aeolic Greek dialect that later Latin-speaking scholars had difficulty understanding. Only one full poem, 'Ode to Aphrodite', survives. The rest are fragments of works that have been copied by ancient scholars or discovered later on strips of papyrus.

Sappho wrote about love, desire, marriage and family using simple, direct language. In the 19th century, Sappho became a role model for women fighting for suffrage, education and autonomy. From the 1960s onward, feminists began identifying her as an icon for love and desire between women due to the probable homoeroticism in some of her surviving fragments. The words 'sapphic' and 'lesbian' to describe love and sex between women both derive from Sappho and the island of her birth.

Surviving fragment of the end of Sappho's first book of collected poems, dated to the second century CE.

Christine de Pizan and the 'City of Ladies'

Considered the first professional female writer in the Western world, Christine de Pizan was born in Venice, Italy, in 1364. Her father, Thomas de Pizan, was a physician and court astrologer to King Charles V of France. Christine originally began her writing career as a way to support her family after her husband died from the plague; however, she soon found success writing love ballads. Her work attracted patrons in the French court, and she was known as a political thinker.

Pizan's most famous work is *The Book of the City of Ladies* (1405), in which she outlined women's societal contributions and argued for their right to an education. The book was translated into Dutch and Portuguese in the 1400s and into English in 1521. In another text, *The Tale of the Rose*, Pizan critiqued the popular book *Romance of the Rose* by Jean de Meun, arguing that Meun unfairly portrayed women as seductresses. In 1429 she published a poem lauding Joan of Arc as a military leader and prophetess. Pizan probably died shortly before Joan's trial and execution.

Detail from *The Book of the City of Ladies*

Artemisia Gentileschi: survival and retribution

Baroque painter Artemisia Gentileschi was born in Rome in 1593. The first female member of the Accademia di Arte del Disegno in Florence, Italy, she became an artist in an era when women were typically deprived of an education and excluded from artistic professions. Moderately successful during her lifetime, today Gentileschi is considered by art critics to be one of the finest artists of her generation.

Gentileschi was trained by her father, artist Orazio Gentileschi, as a teenager. In 1611, her father hired painter Agostino Tassi to mentor her. Instead, Tassi, with an accomplice, raped her. As part of the trial, Gentileschi was tortured with thumbscrews to verify her testimony. Modern feminist scholars have explored her early sexual trauma as strongly influencing Gentileschi's artistic themes of violence and strong women, as portrayed in her painting *Judith Slaying Holofernes*. The majority of her works centre women as protagonists or as subjects on equal footing to men, and many of them feature women who are suffering.

Artemisia Gentileschi's painting *Judith Slaying Holofernes* (c. 1614 to 1620)

Les trois grandes dames of Impressionism

Les trois grandes dames (three great women) of Impressionism were French artists Marie Bracquemond, Berthe Morisot and US artist Mary Cassatt. These women were notable for their contributions to the male-dominated Impressionist movement within an art world hostile to female artists. Morisot was the first female member of the Impressionists. Known for producing small-scale paintings and working in oil paint, watercolour and pastel simultaneously, her paintings depicted everyday life, especially scenes relevant to 19th-century women's lives. Cassatt also focused on everyday scenes, typically of domestic life. Although born in the United States, she lived in France for most of her adult life. Cassatt espoused feminist ideas and, after breaking into the sexist art world of Paris, opened a studio there in 1874. Bracquemond's major works were painted outdoors. Despite her incredible promise and achievements as a woman in the male-dominated Impressionist movement, she abandoned the bulk of her painting career at the urging of her jealous, controlling husband, artist Félix Bracquemond.

Berthe Morisot's *The Sisters*, 1869

Natalie Clifford Barney's salon

Natalie Clifford Barney was born to a wealthy Ohio family in 1876. On moving to Paris, Barney established herself there as queen of the turn-of-the-century lesbian literati, becoming known as a playwright, poet and novelist. She is best known for establishing a salon in Paris's Latin Quarter in 1909, where prominent intellectuals and artists, such as Gertrude Stein, Colette and Auguste Rodin, would gather to exchange ideas and conversation. Barney also established L'Académie des Femmes in 1927, which mentored female writers and served as an alternative to the male-only L'Académie Française.

Fiercely independent and free-spirited throughout her life, Barney is known for living openly and proudly as a lesbian woman during a time when queer women were heavily stigmatized and socially policed. Over the course of her writing career, Barney wrote about feminism, same-sex sexuality, pacifism and paganism. Her epitaph, which she wrote, reads, 'I am this legendary being in which I will live again.'

Natalie Clifford Barney and her dog

Kate Chopin: Southern US feminism

An excerpt from Kate Chopin's 1899 novel *The Awakening* reads, 'She perceived that her will had blazed up, stubborn and resistant. She could not at that moment have done other than denied and resisted. She wondered if her husband had ever spoken to her like that before, and if she had submitted to his command. Of course she had; she remembered that she had. But she could not realize why or how she should have yielded, feeling as she then did.' It points to 19th-century women's oppression in the US South – and the process through which women might reject that oppression, conceiving of themselves as autonomous beings worthy of freedom. Born in St Louis, Missouri, in 1850, Chopin began writing short stories in the 1890s as a way to cope with the deaths of her husband and mother. Her work, which used Louisiana as a backdrop to explore women's self-discovery, female sexuality and Southern racism, was considered offensive and immoral by many critics during her lifetime. In the 1970s, however, Chopin was rediscovered and celebrated as an important Southern voice in feminist literature.

A contemporary of Chopin's, 'Southern belle' Sallie Ward wore cosmetics and risqué outfits. Challenging the norms of society, she married four times. Portrait by Lawrence Hunt Armstrong Downs, 1860.

Edith Wharton on the Gilded Age

New York City novelist, short-story writer and designer Edith Wharton, who wrote over 40 books in as many years, was born into a wealthy family in 1862. In her writing, she was critical of the world in which she grew up, with its extravagant excesses built on the backs of workers. Writing about Gilded Age wealth inequality in her 1905 novel *The House of Mirth*, Wharton declared, 'The dreary limbo of dinginess lay all around and beneath that little illuminated circle in which life reached its finest efflorescence, as the mud and sleet of a winter night enclose a hot-house filled with tropical flowers.' When World War I broke out, Wharton was living in France. She decided to stay and create multiple organizations to help some of the most vulnerable, including schools for children fleeing war in Belgium, hostels for refugees, and establishments for unemployed seamstresses to find work. Wharton also reported on the atrocities of war from the front lines, for which she received the French Legion of Honor. In 1921, Wharton became the first woman to win a Pulitzer Prize for Fiction.

The excesses of the Gilded Age: Marble House, built for
Mr and Mrs William K. Vanderbilt between 1888 and 1892.

The Artists' Suffrage League

A group of female artists founded the UK-based Artists' Suffrage League in 1907. Initially helping to prepare for the National Union of Women's Suffrage Societies' (NUWSS) first mass protest, the group sought to 'further the cause of Women's Enfranchisement by the work and professional help of artists'. In addition to designing posters, the league produced banners for suffrage rallies and marches, pamphlet illustrations and an assortment of suffrage-themed accessories and gifts. Prominent members included chairwoman Mary Lowndes and artist Dora Meeson Coates. Lowndes was a British stained-glass painter influential in the Arts and Crafts movement, and Coates was an Australian oil painter who contributed many of the group's posters. The Artists' Suffrage League was important to feminism for two reasons. First, it brought female artists together who often had to struggle in isolation against the tide of a male-dominated art world. Second, it put the artists' talents to work for an explicitly political cause benefitting women despite the social controversy involved.

Political poster designed by Mary Lowndes for
the Artists' Suffrage League in 1909.

Frida Kahlo: 'I painted my own reality'

Perhaps the most famous feminist artist of all time, Frida Kahlo continues to inspire modern feminists with her vivacious life, body of work and vision for a life of freedom. Born in Mexico City in 1907, she endured extreme pain throughout her life, from a near-fatal, permanently disabling bus accident in 1925 to an abusive marriage with prominent Mexican painter Diego Rivera. However, Kahlo channelled both the pain and the ecstasy of her life into works of artistic brilliance that were ahead of her time. Using vivid, bold colour, she explored themes connected to her harsh reality as a woman in a patriarchal society, from depression and miscarriage to gender equality, bisexuality and colonialism. Kahlo's feminism was grounded in a deep commitment to indigenous Mexican culture as well as in her strong Communist identity. Referring to 'imperialism, fascism, religion, stupidity [and] capitalism' as 'bourgeois tricks', she wrote in her diary, 'I wish to cooperate with the revolution in transforming the world into a classless one, so that we can attain a better rhythm for the oppressed classes.'

Virginia Woolf: 'A Room of One's Own'

In her 1929 extended essay 'A Room of One's Own', English novelist Virginia Woolf wrote, '[A] woman must have money and a room of her own if she is to write fiction. . .' These simple words have resounded with many women, as they express a vision for female independence. In the essay, Woolf emphasized the obstacles women have faced to pursue their creative gifts in a patriarchal society. Women's diminished status, wrote Woolf, has resulted in forced economic reliance on men and disenfranchisement from educational opportunities. To illustrate the extent to which women have been deprived from developing their artistic talents in patriarchal societies, Woolf constructed a thought experiment about Judith Shakespeare, a fictional sister to William Shakespeare. Judith, Woolf argued, may have had the same passion for creative pursuits as William, yet unlike William, Judith's efforts would have been met with scorn and derision by her family and society. Woolf asked her reader to consider how many lost female geniuses there have been as a result of misogyny.

Josephine Baker: 'Black Venus'

Josephine Baker was a tour de force dancer, singer and racial justice activist known for her musical performances during the 1920s and 1930s. Born in St Louis, Missouri, in 1906, Baker grew up in poverty. After learning to sing and dance, she found success on Broadway. She moved to France in the 1920s, where she became one of Europe's highest-paid performers. Baker found that her life was much freer in Paris, as she had experienced brutal anti-black racism and segregation in the United States. During World War II, she joined the resistance movement against the Nazis, driving ambulances and transporting secret messages in her sheet music and underwear. When Baker returned to the United States on tour in the 1950s, she was dismayed to find that the country's racism was still entrenched. Refusing to play at segregated clubs, she became a black civil rights activist. At the 1963 March on Washington she was the only woman to give a speech. When she died in 1975, she was the first US woman to be buried with military honours in France.

Portrait of Josephine Baker in Paris,
by Carl Van Vechten.

Hannah Höch's Weimar Republic art

Weimar-era Germany (1919 to 1933) was a time of cultural flourishing. Lively cabaret and jazz scenes offered urban entertainment, while women adopted short hair and make-up and rebelled against rigid gender expectations. Leftist intellectuals railed against capitalism, hyperinflation and militarism. Conservative reactionaries, meanwhile, expressed displeasure with the modernization and Americanization of Germany, yearning for an idyllic German past that fit their ideology. It was in this raucous environment that German Dada artist Hannah Höch found her inspiration. Höch was one of the inventors of photomontage. Her work explored the idea of the feminist 'New Woman' as well as gender roles, androgyny and politics. In her 1931 piece *Die Starken Männer* (*The Strong Men*), Höch superimposed a sceptical androgynous face over the hypermasculine profile of German boxer Max Schmeling. When the Nazis rose to power, they classified Höch's work as 'degenerate art', and she had to lay low throughout the duration of the Third Reich. After the war, she continued to produce and exhibit her art until her death in 1978.

Hannah Höch (seated), at the grand opening of the first Dada exhibition,
Berlin, 5th June 1920.

Diane Arbus and the social margins

Born into a wealthy Jewish family in New York City in 1923, Diane Arbus became interested in photography, opening a commercial photography business with her husband in 1946. The couple worked as fashion photographers, though Diane grew to hate this. By the mid-1950s, she was photographing strangers on the streets of New York, particularly those from marginalized communities who were considered 'other' by society. Her subjects included disabled people, circus performers, transgender people and nudists.

Arbus is not known to have considered herself a feminist. Still, her unapologetic engagement with groups society shunned is seen by many today as embodying aspects of feminism. As journalist Allison McNearney wrote in 2016, 'Decades before the US would legalize gay marriage, make progress towards transgender rights, start confronting the issues of growing economic inequality, or nominate the first woman for president, Arbus was exploring the artificial boundaries of societal convention versus the truth of living.'

Sylvia Plath's confessional poetry

One month after the 1963 UK publication of her first and only novel, the semi-autobiographical *The Bell Jar*, US poet Sylvia Plath committed suicide at just 30 years old. In the decades since, her work has come to be incorporated into the Western feminist literary canon. A pioneer of confessional poetry, Plath chronicled her struggles with mental illness, the overwhelming demands of motherhood, her abusive marriage, society's unjust expectations and rules for women in the 1950s and 1960s, her authoritarian father and the suicidality that was ever close at hand.

In addition to *The Bell Jar*, Plath published two volumes of poetry during her lifetime: *The Colossus and Other Poems* and *Ariel*. Plath wrote most of the poems in *Ariel* in the last few weeks of her life, giving them a visceral urgency that was later closely analyzed by critics. While Plath's death has often overshadowed her work in popular culture, she remains influential to feminism as a woman who succeeded in defining her own autonomous voice even as she struggled in life.

Sylvia Plath at Smith College c. 1953

Dorothy Allison's *Trash*

Class-based inequality and the experiences of poor and working-class women are common themes in Dorothy Allison's feminist writing. Her works are known for their semi-autobiographical exploration of white rural poverty, childhood abuse, lesbian sexuality and Southern US culture. Her first novel, *Bastard Out of Carolina*, was published in 1992 and has been translated into over a dozen languages. In 1996 it was made into a film.

Allison's 1988 collection *Trash: Short Stories* is widely seen as a defining feminist literary text. In *Trash*, Allison grappled with themes of intergenerational poverty and its connection to despair and abuse within families, in particular between mothers and daughters. She highlighted the power of women's survival and the psychological price of having to make impossible choices. In the short story 'Don't Tell Me You Don't Know', for example, Allison wrote about a man who raped his 11-year-old stepdaughter. The girl's mother 'half hates [him] but can't afford to leave'. *Trash* won two Lambda Literary Awards in 1989.

Dorothy Allison gives a reading as part of the Kelly Writers House Fellowship Program at the University of Pennsylvania in 2015.

The Guerrilla Girls' feminist art activism

The Guerrilla Girls, founded in New York City in 1985, are an anonymous female collective of feminist artists who protest the dearth of female artists and artists of colour in major art galleries and museums. The women's tactics involve putting up posters and billboards, often in the middle of the night, that use statistics on inequality in the art world as well as humour to call out sexist and racist hypocrisy. They're also known for staging public performances. The group's members maintain their anonymity by donning gorilla masks and taking on the names of deceased female artists they consider feminist art icons.

Besides their art-related activism, the Guerrilla Girls have long tackled other issues. They created posters promoting LGBT rights in the 1990s, challenging the racist police brutality that led to the 1992 Los Angeles riots, and supporting the 1992 abortion rights march in Washington, DC. They've also been vocal opponents of the Donald Trump presidency, maintaining a visible presence at the New York and Los Angeles Women's Marches in 2017.

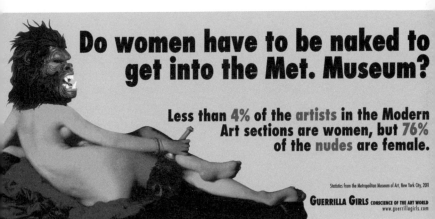

Guerrilla Girls, *Do women have to be naked to get into the Met. Museum?* (2012). The work critiques the hypocrisy of the widespread female nudity in art while work by female artists is severely underrepresented in museums.

Judy Chicago's
The Dinner Party

Created in 1979 by US artist Judy Chicago, *The Dinner Party* is a massive art installation devoted to reclaiming the history of powerful and influential Western women. Chicago set up a large table with three sides and 39 elaborate place settings, each one uniquely decorated to honour a particular woman or goddess written out of her rightful place in history. On porcelain floor tiles beneath the table are written the names of an additional 999 important women associated with those at the table.

US feminist historian Jane Gerhard called the installation 'the most monumental work of the 1970s feminist art movement'. Gerhard argued that the piece transmitted a vision of feminism through art, which was just as important as traditional feminist activism. 'It raised questions,' Gerhard wrote, 'about what constituted "greatness"', including who could create art, what counted as 'high art', and which groups were included in retellings of the past.

Judy Chicago

Angela Carter's feminist fairy tales

In 1979, English writer Angela Carter published a collection of feminist fairy tales titled *The Bloody Chamber*. Influenced by surrealism and the sexual openness of the 1960s, Carter wanted to explore female sexuality in a world in which men's (hetero) sexuality constantly took centre stage. In *The Bloody Chamber* her text championed women's desire 'to re-imagine the world and turn it topsy-turvy', in the words of journalist Michele Roberts. *The Bloody Chamber* injected well-known fairy tales with a self-aware analysis of their sexist ramifications for women. Carter's response to those traditional misogynist tales involved women who made bold choices, who lusted openly and who possessed macabre desires and motives that defied traditional feminine expectations. Carter, however, was apparently uncomfortable with the idea of becoming a highbrow feminist icon. She once said towards the end of her life, 'I had no intention . . . of writing illustrative textbooks of late feminist theory to be used in institutions of education and the thought that I'm taught in universities makes me feel rather miserable.'

Many traditional fairy tales portray women and girls as passive, weak and preyed upon.

Toni Morrison and black women in literature

One of the most prolific and influential novelists in US history, Toni Morrison is the author of multiple novels, such as *The Bluest Eye* (1969), *Sula* (1973) and *Beloved* (1987), which won a Pulitzer Prize in 1988. Central to her work are black women's lives and experiences, including white supremacy and internalized racism, violence against women, poverty, slavery, motherhood and black women's resilience and survival. Her 1992 non-fiction *Playing in the Dark: Whiteness and the Literary Imagination* argued that white canonical writers disparaged blackness in their works in subtle and subconscious ways, and in so doing, established (white) American identity through the rejection of blackness. Despite centring black women in her work, Morrison's connection to feminism is more complicated. In a 1998 interview she stated, 'I think it's off-putting to some readers, who may feel that I'm involved in writing some kind of feminist tract. I don't subscribe to patriarchy, and I don't think it should be substituted with matriarchy. I think it's a question of equitable access, and opening doors to all sorts of things.'

Toni Morrison speaks with
US President Barack Obama
in 2012 as part of receiving the
Presidential Medal of Freedom.

Margaret Atwood's
The Handmaid's Tale

Published in 1985, *The Handmaid's Tale* is a dystopian novel by Canadian Margaret Atwood. It imagines a near-future totalitarian society, the Republic of Gilead, in place of the United States. Based on Christian fundamentalist doctrine, Gilead treats women as the literal property of men. Due to an environmental catastrophe, the remaining fertile women are used as forced reproductive vessels and sex slaves. Women are encouraged to turn against each other in service of the regime, and those who don't comply are tortured and killed. When Donald Trump became president in 2016, with Christian fundamentalist Mike Pence as vice president, feminists incorporated *The Handmaid's Tale* into their activism, donning the handmaidens' red robes and white bonnets to protest political developments they saw as Gilead-esque. Writing in response to whether her novel is a prediction of what's to come in US society, Atwood wrote in 2017, 'Let's say it's an antiprediction: if this future can be described in detail, maybe it won't happen. But such wishful thinking cannot be depended upon either.'

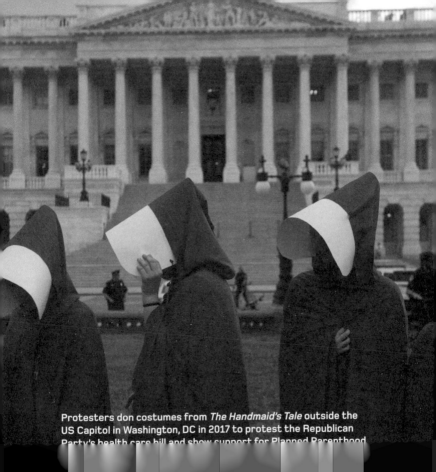

Protesters don costumes from *The Handmaid's Tale* outside the US Capitol in Washington, DC in 2017 to protest the Republican Party's health care bill and show support for Planned Parenthood.

Octavia Butler: Afrofuturist feminism

Science-fiction writer Octavia Butler started writing fiction as a child in southern California. Pursuing her passion, she began to publish short stories and novels in the 1970s. Famous for works such as the explicitly feminist *Kindred* (1979) and *Parable of the Sower* (1993), Butler is known for her visionary work intervening in the white- and male-dominated world of science fiction and injecting it with female characters of colour.

Having grown up exposed to racial discrimination and bullying, Butler highlighted social justice-oriented themes in her stories. These included a critique of social hierarchies and unequal power dynamics; forms of hybridity, from interracial relationships to alien contact that transcends the human form, leading to harmonious mixed communities; and the heroism of marginalized characters forced to sacrifice and persevere. Her work has frequently been associated with Afrofuturism, which combines the study of the African diaspora with technology to uplift blackness and reconceptualize the future from a black perspective.

The Riot Grrrl feminist punk movement

In the 1990s US Northwest, the Riot Grrrl movement – a feminist-fuelled critique of misogyny in the punk music scene as well as in society more generally — was born. Also active in the Washington, DC area, the Riot Grrrl movement emphasized bonds between girls and women (both friendships and romantic relationships) as a way to challenge the internalized sexism and values of competition they had learned from capitalist, Christian, male-dominated society. Kathleen Hanna, lead singer of Riot Grrrl bands Bikini Kill and Le Tigre, was a pivotal figure. Bikini Kill published a zine in 1991 that contained the aptly-named 'Riot Grrrl Manifesto'. Using the language of 'girls', the manifesto reclaimed girlhood from a society that considered girls weak, silly and inconsequential. It spoke of the need to establish music and books created by girls and which centred girls' interests over profits, seeking to 'gain the strength and sense of community that we need in order to figure out how bullshit like racism, able-bodieism [sic], ageism, speciesism, classism, thinism, sexism, anti-semitism and heterosexism figures [sic] in our own lives'.

calling all grrrls and women!
the riot grrrls in and around Washington DC
are organizing a three-day riot grrrl convention
this summer. we invite
all grrrl and feminist bands
and performers, grrrl fanzine
writers, and energetic
grrrls and boys
from across the country
to contribute their skills,
energy, anger, creativity
and curiosity. we will be having
at least three shows, as well as
workshops on everything
from self-defense,
to how to run a
soundboard and
how to lay out a zine.
plus, there will be a lot of
time to talk with
other women about how
we fit (or don't fit!) in
the punk community.

RIOT GRRRL CONVENTION

July 31
August 1
August 2
Washington DC

GO!

we also have
riot grrrl t-shirts
hand-screened by us

pink, red or
white shirts
L or XL
$7 ppd

make t-shirt checks
payable to Kristin Thomson

*what bands
are playing?*

*what else
is going on?*

*where can
I stay?*

riot grrrl!
850 north edison st.
arlington, va 22205
or call
301/935-5463

plus!

riot grrrl #7 is out!
send $1.00 plus 2 stamps
and we'll send you a copy
of our fanzine

1992 Washington, DC-area Riot Grrrl Convention flier.

Persepolis and the Iranian Revolution

Published in the 2000s, *Persepolis* and *Persepolis 2* are autobiographical graphic novels by Iranian-French cartoonist, artist, film director and writer Marjane Satrapi. Originally published in four parts in French, and then later in two parts in English, *Persepolis* explores Satrapi's childhood, adolescence and early adulthood growing up in Tehran, Iran, before, during and after the 1979 Iranian Revolution.

Satrapi uses her perspective as a young girl to narrate the transformation of her society as it became more restrictive and patriarchal towards women in the aftermath of the overthrow of the Shah of Iran. She explores how, raised by a family of Marxist political radicals, she and her family were dismayed by the right-wing fundamentalists who took over the country. Satrapi's work has been praised as sharply analytical, funny, feminist and irreverent. Using a graphic-novel format to explore issues of political power, revolution, gender, class and feminist rebellion has likewise been heralded as fresh and innovative.

A still from the award-winning film version of *Persepolis* (2007). Satrapi was the first woman nominated for an Academy Award for Best Animated Feature.

Deepa Mehta's *Fire*

When Indian-Canadian filmmaker Deepa Mehta's 1996 film *Fire* screened in India in 1998, right-wing Hindu nationalists stormed theatres, tearing down and burning posters, smashing glass and yelling against the film's lesbian content. These attacks set off a firestorm of debate in India over rights to free speech and whether lesbian sexuality was 'alien' to Indian culture. Despite the controversy surrounding its release, *Fire* became a landmark film for Indian lesbian representation.

The film follows the lives of two women, Radha and Sita. Sita has recently married Jatin, who is emotionally distant and carrying on an affair with another woman. The couple live with Jatin's older brother Ashok, a religious ascetic, who is in a sexless marriage with his wife Radha. The film centres on the developing romantic and sexual tension between Sita and Radha. While scholars and critics vary in their appraisal of the film's treatment of gender, sexuality and urban Indian family life, it remains important for its feminist exploration of women's sexual agency.

Shabana Azmi and Nandita Das as Radha and Sita in *Fire*.

Sarah Waters: queer Victorian love

Welsh novelist Sarah Waters brings the worlds of Victorian England, postwar Britain and queer women's subcultures together, in books driven by strong female protagonists that explore themes of romance, sexuality, class, trauma, sex work, incarceration, sexism and political activism. A powerful voice in lesbian, bisexual and queer women's representation in late 20th- and 21st-century literature, she performs extensive research to assure historical accuracy in the fictional worlds she creates.

Waters' first and best-known novel, *Tipping the Velvet*, was published in 1998. Winning multiple awards, including a Lambda Literary Award, it centres on the self-discovery and coming of age of Nancy 'Nan' Astley, an 18-year-old from a working-class English seaside town who becomes infatuated with the male impersonator (drag king) Kitty Butler. Other classic works by Waters include her spiritualist-influenced 1999 novel *Affinity* and the 2002 lesbian crime novel *Fingersmith*.

Pussy Riot : 'Virgin Mary ... Banish Putin'

Based in Moscow since 2011, Russian feminist punk rock group Pussy Riot stages public guerrilla performances to fight against President Vladimir Putin and his dictatorial crackdown on women's rights, LGBTQ rights and freedom of speech. Attempting to play their song 'Punk Prayer' inside a Russian Orthodox church in 2012, members Nadezhda Tolokonnikova, Maria Alyokhina and Yekaterina Samutsevich were arrested and convicted of religious 'hooliganism'. Tolokonnikova and Alyokhina were imprisoned for two years in Siberia and subjected to 'endless humiliations', including forced gynaecological exams, according to Alyokhina.

They've since become prison reform activists and continue to speak out on Putin. The song's lyrics include the following lines: 'Virgin Mary, Mother of God, banish Putin / Banish Putin, banish Putin! . . . Freedom's phantom's gone to heaven / Gay Pride's chained and in detention . . . / Don't upset his Saintship, ladies / Stick to making love and babies. . . / Virgin Mary, Mother of God / Become a feminist, we pray thee.'

Russian punk band Pussy Riot conduct
an anti-Putin action in Red Square,
Moscow, 20th January 2012.

Glossary

Chicana
Term among some Mexican-American women denoting cultural pride, identification with community, emphasis on indigenous ancestry and reclamation from being used as a classist slur; became widely used in the context of the Chicano Movement.

Cisgender
Term used to refer to someone whose gender matches the sex they were assigned at birth; someone who is not transgender.

Decolonization
The cultivation of self-love that rejects damaging ideas about one's racial group or culture imposed by colonizers; unlearning internalized colonization.

Environmental racism
Ways in which human-caused environmental degradation disproportionately impacts communities of colour, especially low-income communities of colour, due to racism and classism; as a term, environmental racism shows how environmentalism, anti-racism and activism against class-based oppression are all connected.

Femicide
A type of gender-based hate crime in which men murder women and girls due to their gender.

Feminism
The belief in gender equality and the liberation of all women from oppression.

Femmephobia
The cultural devaluation of femininity, especially as it applies to queer femme women.

First-wave feminism
The first iteration of the modern feminist movement from the mid-19th century to the early 20th century, focusing primarily on women's suffrage and education rights, the abolition of slavery, violence against women and the temperance movement.

Fourth-wave feminism
Feminism c. 2008–present that centres on intersectionality and sex positivity while making heavy use of the Internet and social media for communication and organizing purposes.

Gender binary
The assumption that sex is synonymous with gender, that the only two genders are male and female, and that all men must be masculine while all women must be feminine.

Global South
Term used in postcolonial studies as a preferential way to describe the so-called 'Third World' or 'developing world'; rejects previous Western-centric terms and their focus on capitalist hierarchical valuation.

Heteronormativity
The assumption that all people are heterosexual and the ways in which that assumption manifests in everyday society.

Intersectionality
The position, coined by US legal scholar and black feminist

Kimberlé Crenshaw in 1991, that feminism must be attentive not just to gender but also to how gender intersects with race and class if it truly hopes to represent the interests of all women. As a theory, intersectionality holds that systems of oppression are overlapping and interlocking.

Latin@, Latinx
Gender-inclusive responses to the word 'Latino'. 'Latin@' was created to include both Latino and Latina within one word, while the more recent 'Latinx' (pronounced 'lah-TEEN-ex') is a move to include non-binary people and challenge the gendered construction of the Spanish language.

LGBTQ+
Lesbian, gay, bisexual, transgender, queer and many other identities falling under this umbrella, such as pansexual and non-binary.

Mestiza
A Latin-American woman whose ancestry is a combination of indigenous and Spanish blood, typically as a result of the violence of colonialism.

Microaggression
The everyday slights and forms of discrimination, whether intentional or unintentional, inflicted on marginalized people, all of which add up to significant psychological distress and

trauma; coined by professor Chester M. Pierce in 1970 in the context of anti-black racism.

Non-binary gender
An experience of gender in which a person doesn't identify as either male or female, or sometimes, as both male and female; a gender identity falling outside the two options of cisgender male or female. Pronouns for non-binary people might be they/them, hir/hirs, or other options.

Objectification
In feminist theory, the way women are reduced from being seen as complex subjects to mere objects of heterosexual male desire.

Othering
The rejection of a group of people from belonging to the in-group; creating an 'us' versus 'them' dynamic among humans in which those deemed 'them' are scapegoated, isolated, ridiculed, dehumanized and often subjected to violence.

Postfeminism
The idea that feminism isn't needed anymore and that women have already achieved equality with men.

Queer
Reclaiming of an anti-gay slur by LGBTQ+ people. Typically used to denote pride in being non-heterosexual and/or non-

cisgender, being committed to a radical, sexually liberatory politics, and as shorthand for LGBTQ+ communities, especially among younger generations.

Rape culture
Feminist sociological term for understanding how, due to misogynist beliefs about gender and sexuality, rape is both pervasive and normalized in society.

Second-wave feminism
Feminism during the 1960s and 1970s, dominated by liberal feminism but also radical feminism, that focused on gender discrimination mainly in the areas of employment, reproductive rights and violence against women; often critiqued as centring the needs of white, class-privileged heterosexual Western feminists to the detriment of other groups of women.

Settler colonialism
A form of colonialism in which the invading population seeks to replace the indigenous population with their own population. Examples of settler colonial societies include the United States, Canada, Australia and New Zealand.

Sex positivity
A feminist movement to reclaim women's right to stigma-free sexual expression and autonomy in the face of patriarchal rape

culture that deems women either 'sluts' or 'prudes'.

'Sex Wars'
Feminist debates active in the 1980s and 1990s (and continuing to the present) about what constitutes feminist sexuality; special emphasis was placed on the feminist ethics (or lack thereof) surrounding sex work, pornography and BDSM (bondage, domination and sadomasochism).

Slut-shaming
The gendered double standards that police and punish women for their real or presumed sexuality; slut-shaming also involves hypersexualizing female bodies, such as calling a teen girl a 'slut' for wearing a short skirt.

Sterilization
A medical procedure conducted in order to eliminate the reproductive capabilities of a human body. While vasectomies, the sterilization procedure typically designed for people with penises, is reversible, tubal ligation ('getting your tubes tied') for people with uteruses is not.

Suffragette
The militant wing of the women's suffrage movement; associated with the British group Women's Social and Political Union founded by Emmeline Pankhurst.

Survivor
Within the context of sexual violence and/or abuse, 'survivor' is often used in place of the older terms 'victim' and 'battered woman' to emphasize resiliency, agency and hope for future healing.

Third-wave feminism
Feminism that emerged in the 1980s and 1990s, largely as a result of the writings of women of colour. Third-wave feminism promoted intersectionality, focusing on the lives of women of colour and poor and working-class women (and the overlap between the two); sex positivity and fighting rape culture; critiquing dominant beauty- and body-based norms; and further incorporating feminist theory into higher education (such as through gay and lesbian studies and postmodern feminism).

Trade union
The banding together of employees as a united front to confront and ameliorate their employer's abuse, discrimination and/or labour exploitation. Acts of solidarity include going on strike (refusing to work) until grievances are addressed, as well as organizing multiple workplaces for action within a specific trade or field.

Transgender
Term used to refer to someone whose gender doesn't match the sex they were assigned at birth; someone who is not cisgender.

Transmisogyny
The specific forms of misogyny directed against transgender women, such as accusing trans women of being insufficiently feminine and thus not 'real' women, or of being too feminine and thus acting as a parody of 'real' women. (A similar term, transmisogynoir, describes the unique forms of oppression directed at black trans women.)

Transphobia
Fear and/or hatred of transgender people, which often manifests as denying the legitimacy of trans people's gender and committing violence against trans people.

Xenophobia
Fear and/or hatred of those deemed 'foreign', such as immigrants.

Zine
Do-it-yourself (DIY) print magazine created by hand and photocopied for comparatively small audiences. Zines have deep historical origins, but became extremely popular in feminist movements beginning with the 1990s Riot Grrrl movement. Feminist zines use personal narrative, art and critiques of popular culture and current events to allow for a general readership to explore social and political issues.

Index

Picture credits

First published in the United States by
Quercus in 2019
Hachette Book Group
1290 Avenue of the Americas
New York, NY 10104

A Hachette UK Company

Copyright © Quercus 2019
Text by Shannon Weber

Edited by Anna Southgate
Designed by Dave Jones
Picture research: Sally Claxton

PB ISBN 9781635061413
EBOOK ISBN 9781635061420